BEYOND OATS

A HORSE LOVER'S COOKBOOK

Have you had your ounce of oats today?
Doctors now have shown
that latest research data proves
what my horse has always known.

This cookbook is a collection of our favorite recipes
which are not necessarily original recipes.

Published by Favorite Recipes Press
P.O. Box 305142
Nashville, TN 37230

First Printing: 1989, 12,500 copies
Manufactured in the United States of America

Library of Congress Number: 89-16901
ISBN: 0-87197-257-3

TABLE OF CONTENTS

ABOUT THE ARTIST

The artist, Chaille (pronounced "Shelley") Groom was born in Chicago, raised in the city of Charleston, South Carolina, and studied art at Stephens College, the University of Colorado and Arizona State University.

Since 1969 her involvement with horses includes training and showing the horses of her grandfather, Ed Tweed, of Brusally Ranch in Scottsdale, Arizona. Chaille's successes in the show ring include top national honors in a wide variety of classes from English and Western Pleasure to sidesaddle, formal driving, cutting, and stock horse. She also has trained and shown horses in dressage, jumping and eventing. These years of experience have proven invaluable to the talented artist who has developed a sensitive and unique style of expression in all media: painting, sketching and writing.

She loves horses and people, and uses her art as a bridge of communication between the two. To Chaille, art is a way of life:

"...to achieve a certain grace, a certain ease, a sensitive combination of feeling and knowledge—is Art, whether it be riding, painting or friendship. This is creativity. Its joy is immeasurable."

Chaille is now married to Elleston Trevor, the author, who wrote among other books The Flight of the Phoenix and who writes the "Quiller" spy novels under the pseudonym of Adam Hall.

ARABIAN HORSE
TRUST

Arabian Horse Trust
12000 Zuni Street
Westminster, Colorado 80234
303/450-4710

To Horse Lovers Everywhere:

The term "horse lover" includes not only owners and breeders, but every man, woman and child who has ever stopped to admire a beautiful horse and marvelled at the grace and symmetry of God's beautiful creation. I am a horse lover, owner and breeder and I also know that horse people love good food. Often an enjoyable meal consists of great food and lots of conversation about—yes—horses. Horse lovers are good people, and our best friends around the world are horse people.

The help and creativity of the many people who contributed their best recipes to this cookbook is an interesting mix and we at the Trust sincerely thank them. This cookbook will be sold by 250 Arabian Horse Clubs across the U.S. and to horse lovers of all breeds and interests around the world. The proceeds of the project will support the heritage, education and research programs of the Arabian Horse Trust and therefore will benefit all breeds and all horse lovers.

Our book contains recipes from our foreign friends who are affiliated with the World Arabian Horse Organization, also from celebrity horse lovers and others involved in some way with horses.

My thanks to Debbie Wilson, Gary Carpenter and Bill Riley of the Trust Staff, and to Ray Ellen Garrison, for their assistance. A very special thanks to Chaille Groom Trevor. Chaille has generously given of her time and talent to help the Arabian Horse Trust. All of the drawings in **Beyond Oats** are hers. Working with her has been a delightful experience.

Thirty years ago I visited my first Arabian Horse Ranch, Brusally Ranch in Scottsdale, Arizona. It was a true oasis in the desert and its owner, Ed Tweed, grandfather of Chaille, made a lasting impression of kindness and integrity. He made Jay and me want to own Arabians.

Enjoy the food and friendship offered in our cookbook and join the fraternity of horse lovers in **Beyond Oats—A Horse Lover's Cookbook**.

Dorothy Stream

Dorothy Stream, Committee Chair
Arabian Horse Trust

LIST OF CONTRIBUTORS

Holly Andersen, Rorbeck Arabians
Willis, Texas . . . . *Pages 74, 161*

Loni Anderson
Jupiter, Florida . . . . *Page 44*

Marie Jo Anderson
Austin, Texas . . . . *Pages 140, 143, 176*

Roberta Ashmore, Rubaiyat Arabians
Loomis, California . . . . *Pages 22, 28, 64, 167*

Ron M. and Sandy Ballantine
Denver, Colorado . . . . *Pages 69, 121*

Clare Donoghue Beck
Goliad, Texas . . . . *Page 170*

Marilyn Bevan, Bevan's Arabians
Rockwall, Texas . . . . *Page 97*

Jennifer Jo Bird, Jen-Mar Arabians
Manor, Texas . . . . *Pages 83, 104, 142, 145, 151*

Theresa Ferland Blaisdell, Thistledown Farm
Lunenburg, Vermont . . . . *Pages 79, 85, 160*

Mr. and Mrs. Brian Blake
Manchester, England . . . . *Page 112*

Vivian Blomquist
Sylmar, California . . . . *Pages 63, 153*

Edwin A. and Shirley Bogucki
Racine, Wisconsin . . . . *Pages 70, 149*

Mrs. Lee Bossen
Clinton, Iowa . . . . *Pages 53, 77*

Ruth Boyd
Denver, Colorado . . . . *Pages 18, 33, 35, 50, 90*

Bart B. Brown
Dallas, Texas . . . . *Page 30*

Bliss Brown, Paramont Arabians
Abingdon, Virginia . . . . *Pages 16, 91, 105, 158*

R. Brown, Aristique Farms
Marion, Indiana . . . . *Page 117*

Robert M. Brunson
Beverly Hills, California . . . . *Pages 53, 67*

When The Sun Comes Up

Breakfast

BREAKFAST SAUSAGE CASSEROLE

This is a Christmas morning tradition at our house.

1½ pounds sausage,
    crumbled
6 slices white bread
3 tablespoons butter,
    softened
2 cups shredded sharp
    Cheddar cheese
5 eggs
2 cups half and half
1 teaspoon dry mustard
1 teaspoon salt

Brown sausage in skillet, stirring until crumbly; drain. Trim bread. Spread with butter. Cut into cubes. Layer bread cubes, sausage and cheese in greased 9x13-inch baking dish. Beat eggs in bowl. Add half and half, dry mustard and salt; mix well. Pour over layers. Chill for 8 hours or longer. Bake at 350 degrees for 40 to 50 minutes or until set and brown. Yield: 10 servings.

Approx Per Serving: *Cal 553; Prot 19.5 g; Carbo 11.6 g; T Fat 47.4 g; Chol 234.0 mg; Potas 276.0 mg; Sod 977.0 mg.*

Bliss Brown, Paramont Arabians
Abingdon, Virginia

CHILI EGG PUFF

Serve on flour tortillas topped with red salsa.

½ cup flour
1 teaspoon baking
    powder
½ teaspoon salt
10 eggs
½ cup melted butter
2 cups cottage cheese
1 pound Monterey Jack
    cheese, shredded
2   4-ounce cans chopped
    green chilies

Mix flour, baking powder and salt in mixer bowl. Add eggs, butter, cottage cheese and Monterey Jack cheese; mix well. Stir in green chilies. Spoon into buttered 9x13-inch baking dish. Bake at 350 degrees for 35 minutes. Yield: 8 servings.

Approx Per Serving: *Cal 506; Prot 29.5 g; Carbo 11.3 g; T Fat 38.0 g; Chol 433.0 mg; Potas 280.0 mg; Sod 875.0 mg.*

Dana C. Ham
Winnemucca, Nevada

EGGS FOR COMPANY

Serve this breakfast casserole with grits.

2 pounds ground sausage
4 cups bread cubes
2 cups shredded sharp
  Cheddar cheese
12 eggs
2 teaspoons dry mustard
2 teaspoons salt
4 cups milk

Brown sausage in skillet, stirring until crumbly; drain. Layer sausage, bread cubes and cheese in greased 10x15-inch baking pan. Beat eggs with dry mustard, salt and milk in mixer bowl. Pour over layers. Chill, covered, for 24 hours. Bake at 350 degrees for 45 minutes. Yield: 12 servings.

Approx Per Serving: *Cal 650; Prot 26.6 g; Carbo 29.7 g; T Fat 46.7 g; Chol 358.0 mg; Potas 397.0 mg; Sod 1324.0 mg.*

Sally Tweed Groom, Brusally Ranch
Scottsdale, Arizona

GRINGO HUEVOS RANCHEROS

I learned this easy way to prepare eggs while stationed at
Fort Bliss, Texas, in the 1930's.

1 4-ounce can chopped
   green chilies, drained
2 tablespoons oil
10 eggs
1 cup shredded
  Monterey Jack cheese
1 cup shredded
  American cheese

Sauté green chilies in oil in large skillet just until warm. Break eggs gently into skillet, taking care not to break yolks. Sprinkle with cheeses. Cook, covered, over medium heat until whites are firm but yolks are still soft. Break yolks with spoon; mix gently. Cook just until soft-set; do not overcook. Serve at once. May substitute chopped fresh peppers for canned peppers if preferred. Yield: 6 servings.

Approx Per Serving: *Cal 462; Prot 28.1 g; Carbo 3.6 g; T Fat 37.1 g; Chol 527.0 mg; Potas 265.0 mg; Sod 859.0 mg.*

General W. O. Kester, D.V.M.
Golden, Colorado

MEXICAN BAKED EGGS

6 corn tortillas
2 tablespoons butter
6 eggs, beaten
1 cup shredded Cheddar
　cheese
1　7-ounce can green
　chili salsa
8 green onions, chopped
8 ounces cottage cheese
8 ounces sour cream

Slice tortillas into 1/8-inch strips. Sauté strips in butter in skillet just until soft. Drain on paper towel. Layer beaten eggs, tortilla strips, cheese, salsa and green onions in 7x10-inch baking dish. Spread with mixture of cottage cheese and sour cream. Bake at 250 degrees for 1 hour. Yield: 6 servings.

Approx Per Serving: *Cal 396; Prot 19.6 g; Carbo 20.0 g; T Fat 27.1 g; Chol 327.0 mg; Potas 362.0 mg; Sod 428.0 mg.*

Debby Wood
Beverly Hills, California

TANGY BAKED EGGS

1 can cream of celery soup
1 can cream of
　mushroom soup
1/2 cup sour cream
6 tablespoons chopped
　green onions
2 tablespoons
　Worcestershire sauce
1/4 cup dry Sherry
2 tablespoons Dijon-
　style mustard
4 teaspoons chopped
　pimento
1/4 teaspoon Tabasco sauce
1/2 teaspoon basil
1/2 teaspoon oregano
12 eggs
1 cup Parmesan cheese
1/2 teaspoon paprika
6 English muffins, split
1/4 cup butter

Combine soups, sour cream, green onions, Worcestershire sauce, Sherry, mustard, pimento, Tabasco sauce, basil and oregano in medium mixer bowl; mix well. Spread in two 9x13-inch baking pans. Break eggs gently into sauce. Sprinkle with Parmesan cheese and paprika. Bake at 325 degrees for 25 minutes or just until whites are set. Spread muffin halves with butter. Toast until light brown. Place on serving plates. Lift each egg gently onto muffin half; spoon sauce over top. Serve immediately. Yield: 12 servings.

Approx Per Serving: *Cal 287; Prot 12.2 g; Carbo 19.0 g; T Fat 17.3 g; Chol 287.0 mg; Potas 168.0 mg; Sod 796.0 mg.*

Ruth Boyd
Denver, Colorado

OVEN OMELET

Serve this easy dish to weekend horse show guests.

1/4 cup margarine
18 eggs
1 cup sour cream
1 cup milk
2 teaspoons salt
1/4 cup chopped green
　onions
1 cup chopped ham
1 cup shredded Cheddar
　cheese
1 cup sliced mushrooms

Melt margarine in 9x13-inch baking dish. Beat eggs, sour cream, milk and salt in mixer bowl until smooth. Stir in green onions, ham, cheese and mushrooms. Pour into prepared baking dish. Bake at 325 degrees for 35 minutes or until set in center but still moist. Yield: 12 servings.

Approx Per Serving: *Cal 290; Prot 16.0 g; Carbo 3.3 g; T Fat 23.6 g; Chol 442.0 mg; Potas 244.0 mg; Sod 839.0 mg.*

Janice Merlino
Phoenix, Arizona

TWENTY-FOUR HOUR OMELET

I got this recipe from Mrs. Glover R. Baldock.

8 slices white sandwich
　bread
1/4 cup butter, softened
1 pound longhorn
　cheese, shredded
1/4 cup chopped green
　onions
1 cup sliced fresh
　mushrooms
8 eggs
3 cups milk
3/4 teaspoon dry mustard
3/4 teaspoon salt
Cayenne pepper to taste

Spread bread with butter. Cut into 1-inch cubes. Layer bread cubes, cheese, green onions and mushrooms in greased 9x13-inch baking dish. Beat eggs, milk and seasonings in mixer bowl. Pour over layers. Chill for 6 hours or longer. Bake, covered, at 350 degrees for 1 hour. Bake, uncovered, for 5 minutes longer or until light brown. Yield: 8 servings.

Approx Per Serving: *Cal 492; Prot 25.8 g; Carbo 19.9 g; T Fat 34.3 g; Chol 362.0 mg; Potas 318.0 mg; Sod 852.0 mg.*

Bazy Tankersley
Tucson, Arizona

STUFFED FRENCH TOAST

1/2 cup chopped onion
8 ounces hot sausage
2 tablespoons butter
4 ounces cream cheese,
  softened
1/4 teaspoon salt
1/2 teaspoon pepper
4 slices bacon, crisp-
  fried, crumbled
1 loaf unsliced bread
6 eggs, beaten
1/2 cup (about) milk

Sauté onion and sausage in butter in skillet, stirring until sausage is brown and crumbly; drain. Combine with cream cheese, salt, pepper and bacon in bowl; mix well. Cut bread into slices, making every other cut to but not through bottom to form pockets. Spoon 2½ tablespoons sausage mixture into each pocket. Dip filled slices into mixture of eggs and milk as for French toast. Cook in a small amount of oil on grill until brown on both sides. Garnish with paprika. Serve with warm maple syrup. Yield: 8 servings.

Approx Per Serving: *Cal 509; Prot 17.5 g; Carbo 43.8 g; T Fat 28.8 g; Chol 253.0 mg; Potas 271.0 mg; Sod 863.0 mg.*
Nutritional information does not include oil for browning toast.

Linda Stream
San Luis Obispo, California

BANANA OAT BREAKFAST CAKE

5 tablespoons melted
  butter
1 package coconut pecan
  frosting mix
1 cup oats
1 cup sour cream
4 eggs
2 large bananas, chopped
1 2-layer package
  yellow cake mix

Combine butter, dry frosting mix and oats in bowl; mix well. Set aside. Beat sour cream, eggs and bananas in mixer bowl until smooth. Add cake mix; beat at medium speed for 2 minutes. Layer batter and oats mixture 1/3 at a time in greased 10-inch tube pan. Bake at 375 degrees for 50 to 60 minutes or until cake tests done. Cool in pan for 15 minutes. Remove to wire rack to cool completely. Yield: 16 servings.

Approx Per Serving: *Cal 313; Prot 4.4 g; Carbo 44.6 g; T Fat 13.3 g; Chol 84.6 mg; Potas 112.0 mg; Sod 285.0 mg.*

Betty Zekan
Richfield, Ohio

CINNAMON SURPRISE

This is a light change from heavy pastries and cinnamon rolls.

2   8-count packages
    refrigerator crescent roll
    dough
2 tablespoons brown
    sugar
1 teaspoon sugar
1 teaspoon cinnamon
16 marshmallows
2 tablespoons melted
    butter

Separate roll dough on lightly floured surface. Mix brown sugar, sugar and cinnamon in small bowl. Dip marshmallows 1 at a time in melted butter; roll in sugar mixture, coating well. Place on triangle of roll dough. Bring up edges to enclose marshmallow, sealing well. Place 2 inches apart on baking sheet. Brush lightly with remaining melted butter. Bake at 375 degrees for 10 to 13 minutes or until marshmallows melt, leaving rolls with hollow, sweet-coated centers. Yield: 16 servings.

Approx Per Serving: *Cal 143; Prot 1.7 g; Carbo 18.8 g; T Fat 6.9 g; Chol 3.9 mg; Potas 70.1 mg; Sod 249.0 mg.*

Lynne Sebelius Halpenny
Bieber, California

GRAND CHAMPION BLUEBERRY MUFFINS

These muffins won the Grand Prize at my 1986 county fair.

1/2 cup butter, softened
1 cup sugar
2 eggs
1 teaspoon vanilla extract
2 teaspoons baking
    powder
1/4 teaspoon salt
2 cups flour
1/2 cup milk
2 1/2 cups fresh
    blueberries
1 tablespoon sugar
1/2 teaspoon nutmeg

Cream butter in mixer bowl until light. Add 1 cup sugar, beating until fluffy. Beat in eggs 1 at a time. Add vanilla, baking powder and salt; mix well. Add flour and milk 1/2 at a time, mixing gently after each addition. Fold in blueberries. Spoon into paper-lined muffin cups. Sprinkle with mixture of 1 tablespoon sugar and nutmeg. Bake at 375 degrees for 25 to 30 minutes or until golden brown. May substitute one 12-ounce bag thawed frozen blueberries for fresh if preferred. Yield: 18 muffins.

Approx Per Muffin: *Cal 245; Prot 3.8 g; Carbo 37.5 g; T Fat 9.3 g; Chol 67.7 mg; Potas 75.0 mg; Sod 182.0 mg.*

Nanci Lee Sorenson-Harvey
Lake Geneva, Wisconsin

BRAN MUFFINS

This is an original recipe developed 15 years ago during a health kick.

1 cup whole wheat flour
1 teaspoon soda
1/2 cup whole bran
1 egg
1/2 cup dark molasses
3/4 cup milk
2 teaspoons butter,
  softened
1/2 cup golden raisins
1/2 cup chopped pecans

Mix whole wheat flour, soda, bran, egg, molasses, milk and butter in mixer bowl; mix well. Stir in raisins and pecans. Spoon into paper-lined muffin cups. Bake at 350 degrees for 15 to 20 minutes or until muffins test done.

Variation: E. E. Hurlbutt of Calarabia in Santa Clarita, California, makes Oat Bran Muffins by adding 1 1/2 cups oat bran, 1/4 cup oil and 1/4 cup pineapple juice to this basic recipe and substitutes walnuts for pecans.
Yield: 24 muffins.

Approx Per Muffin: *Cal 70; Prot 1.6 g; Carbo 11.2 g; T Fat 2.6 g; Chol 13.3 mg; Potas 271.0 mg; Sod 50.0 mg.*
Nutritional information is for Bran Muffins only.

Roberta Ashmore, Rubaiyat Arabians
Loomis, California

MOTHER'S BRAN MUFFINS

This is a good muffin for a diet.

4 cups All-Bran
2 cups 100% bran
2 cups boiling water
1/2 cup shortening
1 tablespoon honey
1 cup packed brown
  sugar
5 egg whites, slightly
  beaten
4 cups buttermilk
5 cups whole wheat flour
5 teaspoons soda
1 teaspoon salt
1 cup raisins
1 cup chopped walnuts
1 cup chopped dates

Mix All-Bran and 100% bran in bowl. Stir in boiling water. Let stand for several minutes. Cream shortening, honey and brown sugar in mixer bowl until light and fluffy. Mix in egg whites and buttermilk. Add to bran mixture; mix well. Add mixture of sifted flour, soda and salt; mix well. Stir in raisins, walnuts and dates. Store in refrigerator for up to 4 weeks. Spoon into greased muffin cups. Bake at 400 degrees for 15 to 18 minutes or until brown.
Yield: 60 muffins.

Approx Per Muffin: *Cal 120; Prot 3.7 g; Carbo 22.3 g; T Fat 3.5 g; Chol 0.6 mg; Potas 226.0 mg; Sod 208.0 mg.*

Joyce Gardner
Bend, Oregon

OAT BRAN MUFFINS

2 cups oat bran
1/4 cup packed brown
  sugar
1 tablespoon soy flour
2 teaspoons baking
  powder
1/2 teaspoon salt
1 cup milk
2 eggs, slightly beaten
1/4 cup honey
2 tablespoons oil
2 bananas, mashed
1/2 cup chopped pecans

Mix oat bran, brown sugar, soy flour, baking powder and salt in bowl. Add milk, eggs, honey and oil; mix just until moistened. Stir in bananas and pecans. Spoon into greased muffin cups. Bake at 425 degrees for 15 to 17 minutes or until brown. Yield: 12 muffins.

Approx Per Muffin: *Cal 173; Prot 5.2 g; Carbo 27.5 g; T Fat 8.1 g; Chol 48.4 mg; Potas 249.0 mg; Sod 170.0 mg.*

Judy Nordquist
Evergreen, Colorado

MORNING GLORY MUFFINS

This easy and nutritious recipe is from my sister.

2 cups flour
1 1/4 cups sugar
2 teaspoons soda
2 teaspoons cinnamon
1/2 teaspoon salt
2 cups grated carrots
1/2 cup coconut
1/2 cup raisins
1 apple, grated
1/2 cup chopped pecans
3 eggs
2 teaspoons vanilla
  extract

Mix flour, sugar, soda, cinnamon and salt in bowl. Mix in carrots, coconut, raisins, apple and pecans. Add eggs and vanilla; mix well. Spoon into greased muffin cups. Bake at 350 degrees for 20 minutes. May substitute whole wheat flour for part of the flour if preferred. Yield: 12 muffins.

Approx Per Muffin: *Cal 322; Prot 5.0 g; Carbo 54.2 g; T Fat 10.6 g; Chol 68.5 mg; Potas 233.0 mg; Sod 292.0 mg.*

Patricia Trapp
Big Bend, Wisconsin

CALARABIA PANCAKES

Serve with ham or little pork sausages.

4 egg yolks, beaten
1/2 cup pineapple juice
1/2 cup flour
4 egg whites
1 20-ounce can
  pineapple tidbits
Arrowroot
1 tablespoon butter
1 tablespoon lemon juice

Combine egg yolks, pineapple juice and flour in bowl; mix well. Beat egg whites in mixer bowl until stiff peaks form. Fold gently into pancake batter. Bake on oiled griddle until light brown on both sides. Mix undrained pineapple with enough arrowroot for desired consistency in saucepan. Cook until thickened, stirring constantly. Stir in butter and lemon juice. Serve on pancakes. Yield: 4 servings.

Approx Per Serving: *Cal 290; Prot 8.4 g; Carbo 45.7 g; T Fat 8.8 g; Chol 282.0 mg; Potas 274.0 mg; Sod 96.3 mg.*
Nutritional information does not include arrowroot.

E. E. Hurlbutt, Calarabia
Santa Clarita, California

HEARTLAND'S "FILLY" WAFFLES

This recipe was developed to serve at the celebration of the birth of a filly at Heartland. I serve it twice a week during the foaling season now.

2 cups sifted flour
2 teaspoons baking
  powder
3/4 teaspoon salt
3 egg yolks, beaten
1/3 cup oil
13/4 cups milk
3 egg whites

Mix flour, baking powder and salt in bowl. Combine egg yolks, oil and milk in mixer bowl; mix well. Mix in dry ingredients. Beat egg whites in mixer bowl until stiff peaks form. Fold gently into batter; do not overmix. Pour 7/8 cup at a time into Belgian waffle iron. Bake for 4 minutes or according to manufacturer's instructions. Serve with butter, syrup, cream or ice cream. May substitute 3 tablespoons baking cocoa for 3 tablespoons flour for chocolate lovers. Yield: 6 waffles.

Approx Per Waffle: *Cal 331; Prot 9.4 g; Carbo 33.1 g; T Fat 17.5 g; Chol 147.0 mg; Potas 166.0 mg; Sod 441.0 mg.*

Jayne D. Solberg, Heartland Farms
Baltic, South Dakota

Just A Bit

Appetizers and Beverages

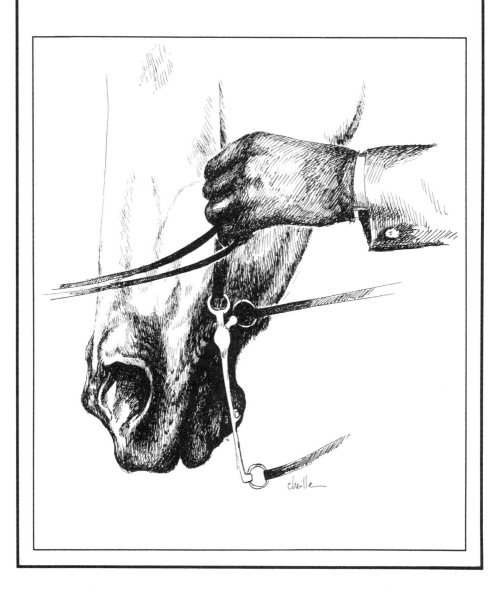

WAYNE'S FAVORITE STUFFED MUSHROOMS

24 large mushrooms
1¹/₂ cups seasoned dry
  bread crumbs
1 cup flaked cooked
  crab meat
¹/₂ cup finely chopped
  onion
¹/₂ cup finely shredded
  Colby cheese
¹/₂ cup cream
1 cup finely shredded
  Colby cheese

Remove mushroom stems. Rinse mushroom caps; pat dry. Combine dry bread crumbs, crab meat, onion, ¹/₂ cup cheese and salt and pepper to taste in bowl. Add cream; mix lightly. Spoon into mushroom caps. Arrange in shallow glass baking dish. Top each mushroom with about 2 teaspoons cheese. Bake at 350 degrees for 10 to 15 minutes. Yield: 24 appetizers.

Nutritional information is not available.

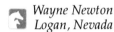 *Wayne Newton*
Logan, Nevada

ARABIAN EGGPLANT DIP

1 large round eggplant
2 or 3 cloves of garlic
1 teaspoon (about) salt
¹/₄ cup tahinah
¹/₄ cup lemon juice
Olive oil
Chopped parsley
1 red bell pepper, sliced
Red pepper to taste

Bake eggplant in hot oven or sear over open flame until eggplant is tender and skin is blackened. Rinse with cold water. Peel and chop into small pieces. Mash garlic with enough salt to equal volume of garlic in bowl until consistency of paste. Add eggplant. Mash until smooth. Add tahinah and lemon juice; mix well. Spoon into serving bowl. Drizzle olive oil over top. Sprinkle with parsley. Arrange red pepper slices over parsley. Sprinkle with red pepper. Omit tahinah for Turkish-style dip. Yield: 5 servings.

Nutritional information is not available.

*Excerpted from **Aramco World***

CREAM CHEESE BALL

Everyone will ask "What is in this cheese ball?"

1 15-ounce can fruit
   cocktail
16 ounces cream cheese,
   softened
1 4-ounce package
   French vanilla instant
   pudding mix
2 tablespoons orange
   juice
1 cup slivered almonds

Pour fruit cocktail into colander. Let drain for 2 hours. Blend cream cheese, pudding mix and orange juice in bowl. Add fruit cocktail; mix well. Shape into ball. Roll in almonds to coat. Place on serving plate. Chill for several hours. Serve with assorted crackers. Yield: 8 servings.

Approx Per Serving: *Cal 416; Prot 7.8 g; Carbo 35.4 g; T Fat 28.7 g; Chol 61.9 mg; Potas 247.0 mg; Sod 315.0 mg.*

Gail Cohan, Dynasty Arabians II, Inc.
Delray Beach, Florida

KILLER JELLY WITH CREAM CHEESE

Keep the telephone number of the local fire department handy.

7 jalapeño peppers,
   seeded
4 relleno peppers, seeded
1¹/₂ cups cider vinegar
2¹/₂ pounds sugar
6 ounces liquid pectin
8 ounces cream cheese,
   softened

Place peppers in food processor container. Process with steel blade until minced. Combine peppers, vinegar and sugar in large saucepan. Bring to a boil, stirring constantly; reduce heat. Simmer for 10 minutes; skim. Stir in pectin. Bring to a boil. Boil for 1 minute; remove from heat. Place in large container; seal tightly. Store in refrigerator. Mold cream cheese into decorative shape. Place on serving plate. Spoon generous amount of jelly over cream cheese. Serve with Triscuits. Yield: 1 recipe.

Nutritional information is not available.

T. G. Cyn
Gainesville, Virginia

AVOCADO AND SALMON SPREAD

1 large avocado, mashed
1 8-ounce can salmon, drained, mashed
1/2 cup ricotta cheese
1/4 cup thinly sliced green onion
1 green bell pepper, seeded, finely chopped
1 1/2 teaspoons garlic salt
2 teaspoons prepared mustard
1 teaspoon prepared horseradish
1/8 teaspoon lemon pepper
Alfalfa sprouts to taste

Combine avocado, salmon, ricotta cheese, green onion, green pepper, garlic salt, mustard, horseradish and lemon pepper in bowl; mix well. Spoon into serving bowl. Garnish with light sprinkling of alfalfa sprouts. Serve with assorted crackers and alfalfa sprouts on the side. Yield: 48 tablespoons.

Approx Per Tablespoon: *Cal 19; Prot 1.4 g; Carbo 0.6 g; T Fat 1.3 g; Chol 3.9 mg; Potas 57.0 mg; Sod 74.2 mg.*
Nutritional information does not include alfalfa sprouts.

Marilynn Hajek
Longmont, Colorado

HOT CRAB DIP

16 ounces cream cheese, softened
1 cup mayonnaise
1 pound imitation crab meat
1 teaspoon prepared horseradish sauce
1/8 teaspoon Worcestershire sauce
1/8 teaspoon paprika

Blend cream cheese and mayonnaise in bowl. Add crab meat; mix well. Add horseradish sauce and Worcestershire sauce; mix well. Place in 9x11-inch baking dish sprayed with nonstick cooking spray. Sprinkle with paprika. Bake at 375 degrees for 15 minutes. Reduce oven temperature to 350 degrees. Bake for 30 minutes longer. Yield: 40 servings.

Approx Per Serving: *Cal 91; Prot 2.3 g; Carbo 1.6 g; T Fat 8.5 g; Chol 17.9 mg; Potas 26.5 mg; Sod 160.0 mg.*

Roberta Ashmore, Rubaiyat Arabians
Loomis, California

28

GUACAMOLE

This dip is different than most, as it is chunky. A former resident of New Mexico gave it to me many years ago.

4 avocados
1/2 lemon
1/4 teaspoon salt
1 onion, finely chopped
2 tomatoes, chopped
1/4 cup Worcestershire
  sauce
1 tablespoon Tabasco
  sauce
1 pound longhorn
  cheese, shredded

Cut avocados into halves lengthwise. Remove seed. Squeeze lemon juice over cut avocados. Peel. Combine avocados and salt in bowl; mash coarsely. Add onion and tomatoes; mix well. Stir in Worcestershire sauce and Tabasco sauce. Fold in cheese. Chill until serving time. Yield: 8 servings.

Approx Per Serving: *Cal 410; Prot 16.8 g; Carbo 12.7 g; T Fat 34.3 g; Chol 59.8 mg; Potas 818.5 mg; Sod 513.0 mg.*

Jane L. Hall
Chino, California

"AFTER THE SHOW" CON QUESO

The beauty of this recipe is that it can be made in the morning before you go to the morning classes. Turn it on when you return in the evening, and by the time you have the margaritas served, you've got a great light supper, or a wonderful appetizer for the victory celebration!

2 pounds lean ground
  beef
2 pounds Velveeta
  cheese with chilies,
  cubed
2 onions, chopped
4 hot peppers, minced
2 14-ounce cans peeled
  tomatoes
1/8 teaspoon Tabasco
  sauce

Brown ground beef in skillet, stirring until crumbly; drain. Spoon into Crock•Pot. Add cheese, onions, hot peppers, tomatoes and Tabasco sauce; mix well. Cook, covered, on High for 1 hour. Serve with tortilla chips. Yield: 6 cups.

Approx Per Cup: *Cal 854; Prot 57.9 g; Carbo 22.8 g; T Fat 58.0 g; Chol 195.0 mg; Potas 1293.0 mg; Sod 1764.0 mg.*

Misdee Wilson, Kaaba Arabian Enterprises
Scottsdale, Arizona

SPINACH AND SHRIMP DIP

1 10-ounce package
frozen spinach, thawed,
drained
1½ cups sour cream
1 cup mayonnaise
1 envelope dry Swiss
Leek soup mix
1 bunch green onions,
chopped
1 8-ounce can sliced
water chestnuts,
drained, chopped
1 cup shrimp
¼ teaspoon Dijon
mustard
5 drops of Tabasco sauce
1 large round loaf
sourdough bread

Squeeze spinach dry. Place in large bowl. Add sour cream, mayonnaise, soup mix, onions, water chestnuts, shrimp, mustard and Tabasco sauce, mixing well after each addition. Chill for 2 hours. Cut top from bread; hollow out loaf to make shell. Spoon shrimp mixture into bread shell. Serve immediately. Yield: 48 tablespoons.

Approx Per Tablespoon: *Cal 89; Prot 2.5 g; Carbo 7.1 g; T Fat 5.8 g; Chol 15.3 mg; Potas 59.5 mg; Sod 185.0 mg.*

Barbara McKenzie
Bellevue, Washington

NEILS CREEK SOUR CREAM DIP

Serve this dip with corn chips. It is also good on baked potatoes and even better the second day.

Juice of 1 lemon
16 ounces sour cream
1 onion, chopped
8 jalapeño peppers,
seeded, chopped
2 cloves of garlic, minced
2 sprigs of cilantro,
chopped

Combine lemon juice and sour cream in mixer bowl; mix well. Add onion and peppers; mix well. Add garlic and cilantro, mixing well after each addition. Chill until serving time. Serve with corn chips. Yield: 48 tablespoons.

Approx Per Tablespoon: *Cal 22; Prot 0.4 g; Carbo 0.9 g; T Fat 2.0 g; Chol 4.2 mg; Potas 22.8 mg; Sod 25.9 mg.*

Bart B. Brown
Dallas, Texas

PANCHO VILLA'S TACO DIP

3 ripe avocados
2 tablespoons lime juice
1/2 teaspoon salt
1/2 teaspoon pepper
1 cup sour cream
1/2 cup mayonnaise
1 envelope dry taco
  seasoning mix
2 10-ounce cans bean dip
1 10-ounce can chopped
  jalapeño peppers
1 cup chopped scallions
3 tomatoes, chopped
1 4-ounce can chopped
  olives
8 ounces sharp orange
  Cheddar cheese,
  shredded

Mash avocados in small bowl. Sprinkle with lime juice, salt and pepper; mix well. Combine sour cream, mayonnaise and taco seasoning mix in bowl; mix well. Spread bean dip into bottom of 9-inch glass dish. Arrange layers of jalapeño peppers, avocado mixture, sour cream mixture, scallions, tomatoes, olives and cheese over bean dip layer. Chill until serving time. Serve with dip-size corn chips or tortilla chips. *Peter R. Sarra of Canton, Massachussetts* uses a mixture of Monterey Jack and Cheddar cheeses. Yield: 50 servings.

Approx Per Serving: *Cal 91; Prot 2.6 g; Carbo 5.8 g; T Fat 6.8 g; Chol 8.1 mg; Potas 168.0 mg; Sod 382.0 mg.*

Nell B. and W. C. "Dub" Miller
Dallas, Texas

ARTICHOKES VINAIGRETTE

This could also be prepared as individual salads or as a buffet salad.

1/2 cup oil
1/4 cup tarragon vinegar
1 teaspoon salt
1/2 teaspoon pepper
1 teaspoon paprika
1/2 teaspoon dry mustard
1/8 teaspoon tarragon
2 large artichokes,
  cooked, chilled
3 hard-boiled eggs
1/2 onion, minced
2 tablespoons fresh
  parsley, chopped
2 tablespoons capers

Combine oil, vinegar, and seasonings in bowl; mix well. Chill overnight. Arrange artichoke leaves around shallow bowl or on serving platter. Chill for several hours. Remove and discard thistle from artichoke hearts; chop hearts. Place in bowl. Cut eggs in half; reserve yolks. Chop egg whites. Add egg whites and onion to artichoke hearts; mix well. Press reserved egg yolks through sieve. Add to egg white mixture. Add parsley and capers; toss lightly. Spoon mixture onto center of artichoke leaves. Stir dressing to mix well. Drizzle over egg mixture and artichoke leaves. Serve. Yield: 1 recipe.

Approx Per Recipe: *Cal 1353; Prot 25.3 g; Carbo 38.6 g; T Fat 127.0 g; Chol 822.0 mg; Potas 1127.0 mg; Sod 2503.0 mg.*

Ruth Husband
Brea, California

BEEF JERKY

1 pound lean round steak
1/4 cup soy sauce
1/4 cup Worcestershire
  sauce
1 tablespoon catsup
1/4 teaspoon pepper
1/4 teaspoon garlic
  powder
1/4 teaspoon onion
  powder
1/4 teaspoon salt
1 teaspoon liquid
  hickory smoke

Place round steak in freezer for 45 minutes or until partially frozen. Slice round steak with the grain into 1/4-inch strips. Combine soy sauce, Worcestershire sauce, catsup, pepper, garlic powder, onion powder, salt and liquid smoke in large bowl; mix well. Place steak strips into marinade. Marinate for 2 hours to overnight. Pour mixture into colander; drain well. Place steak strips on 10x15-inch baking sheet. Bake at 150 degrees for 8 to 10 hours until strips "bend like a green willow." Yield: 1 pound.

Nutritional information is not available.

Jim Reno
Riverside, California

CHEESE RYES

2 cups shredded sharp
  Cheddar cheese
1 cup mayonnaise
2 tablespoons chopped
  onion
1 4-ounce jar stuffed
  olives, drained,
  chopped
1 loaf party rye bread

Combine cheese, mayonnaise, onion and olives in bowl; mix well. Spread on rye bread slices. Arrange on foil-lined 10x15-inch baking sheet. Broil just until brown and bubbly. Serve immediately. Yield: 30 appetizers.

Approx Per Appetizer: *Cal 129; Prot 3.3 g; Carbo 7.7 g; T Fat 9.7 g; Chol 12.3 mg; Potas 42.7 mg; Sod 223.0 mg.*

Ruth Mawby
Augusta, Michigan

TOASTED ONION CANAPÉS

3/4 cup chopped onion
1/2 cup mayonnaise
1/4 cup Parmesan cheese
24 crackers

Combine onion, mayonnaise and cheese in bowl; mix well. Spread on crackers. Place on baking sheet. Broil just until golden brown. Serve hot. Yield: 24 canapés.

Approx Per Canapé: *Cal 51; Prot 0.6 g; Carbo 2.7 g; T Fat 4.2 g; Chol 4.4 mg; Potas 14.5 mg; Sod 80.6 mg.*

Mary Jane Parkinson
El Cajon, California

CHEESE AND SPINACH PUFFS

1   10-ounce package frozen chopped spinach, thawed
1/2 cup chopped onion
2 eggs, slightly beaten
1/2 cup Parmesan cheese
1/2 cup shredded Cheddar cheese
1/2 cup blue cheese salad dressing
1/4 cup margarine, melted
1/2 teaspoon garlic powder
1   8-ounce package corn muffin mix

Combine spinach and onion in glass bowl. Microwave on High until tender. Drain well; squeeze dry. Combine eggs, cheeses, salad dressing, margarine and garlic powder in bowl; mix well. Add spinach mixture and corn muffin mix; mix well. Chill, covered, for several hours. Shape into 1-inch balls. Chill or freeze, wrapped, until serving time. Place on 10x15-inch baking sheet. Bake chilled puffs at 350 degrees for 10 to 12 minutes or frozen puffs for 12 to 15 minutes. Serve hot. Yield: 60 puffs.

Approx Per Puff: *Cal 33; Prot 1.0 g; Carbo 1.9 g; T Fat 2.4 g; Chol 11.4 mg; Potas 24.9 mg; Sod 59.3 mg.*

Ruth Boyd
Denver, Colorado

MARGIE'S PINWHEELS

8 ounces cream cheese,
  softened
1/4 cup sour cream
3 green onions, chopped
1 1/2 jalapeño peppers,
  seeded, finely chopped
10 flour tortillas

Combine cream cheese, sour cream, onions and peppers in bowl; mix well. Place 3 or 4 tortillas at a time on paper plate. Microwave for 30 seconds or until warm. Spread warm tortillas with cream cheese mixture. Roll as for jelly roll; wrap tightly in plastic wrap. Chill overnight. Cut into slices. Yield: 10 servings.

Approx Per Serving: *Cal 198; Prot 4.5 g; Carbo 20.5 g; T Fat 11.8 g; Chol 27.3 mg; Potas 85.5 mg; Sod 229.0 mg.*

Mrs. Robert Kennaugh, Manx Farms
Corsicana, Texas

MUSHROOM HORS D'OEUVRES

These freeze well before baking. I keep a batch in the freezer at all times so when guests stop over I always have something tasty ready to serve.

1 pound mushrooms,
  finely chopped
1 onion, finely chopped
1/4 cup butter, softened
12 ounces cream cheese,
  softened
1 1/2 teaspoons
  Worcestershire sauce
1/4 teaspoon garlic salt
1   16-ounce loaf
  Pepperidge Farm thinly
  sliced white bread
1/4 cup butter, softened
1/4 cup Parmesan cheese

Sauté mushrooms and onion in butter in skillet until onions are transparent. Add cream cheese, Worcestershire sauce and garlic salt; mix well. Spread over 10 bread slices. Butter 1 side of 10 bread slices. Place butter side up on mushroom mixture. Sprinkle with Parmesan cheese. Cut each sandwich into quarters. Arrange on 10x15-inch baking sheet. Bake at 350 degrees for 10 minutes or until mixture is bubbly. Yield: 40 small sandwiches.

Approx Per Sandwich: *Cal 87; Prot 2.1 g; Carbo 6.6 g; T Fat 5.9 g; Chol 15.9 mg; Potas 73.8 mg; Sod 127.0 mg.*

Judy Fojtik
Ingleside, Illinois

SPANOKOPETA

2 bunches green onions, chopped
1 cup butter
3 cups cottage cheese
1 teaspoon salt
1 teaspoon pepper
1 teaspoon dillseed
1 teaspoon garlic powder
1/2 teaspoon instant minced onion
4 16-ounce packages frozen spinach, thawed, drained
4 ounces Cheddar cheese, shredded
1/8 teaspoon garlic salt
Chopped parsley
1 package phyllo dough

Sauté green onions in butter in skillet until clear. Combine cottage cheese, salt, pepper, dillseed, garlic powder and instant onion in large bowl; mix well. Add spinach and green onions; mix well. Combine Cheddar cheese, garlic salt and parsley in bowl. Alternate layers of phyllo, cottage cheese mixture and light sprinkling of Cheddar cheese mixture in 9x13-inch baking dish, ending with phyllo. Bake at 350 degrees for 20 minutes or until phyllo is golden brown. Yield: 24 servings.

Approx Per Serving: *Cal 162; Prot 8.8 g; Carbo 10.2 g; T Fat 10.7 g; Chol 29.9 mg; Potas 495.0 mg; Sod 378.0 mg.*
Nutritional information does not include phyllo dough.

Ruth Boyd
Denver, Colorado

SPICY CHICKEN WINGS

12 chicken wings
1 12-ounce bottle of beer
1 5-ounce bottle of Tabasco sauce
1 18-ounce bottle of hot and spicy barbecue sauce

Wash chicken wings. Disjoint wings; discard tips. Place in large saucepan. Add beer and Tabasco sauce. Bring to a boil; reduce heat. Simmer for 20 minutes or until chicken is tender. Dilute barbecue sauce with a small amount of water. Dip chicken into sauce; arrange on 10x15-inch baking sheet. Broil for 5 minutes on each side. Serve hot. Yield: 12 servings.

Approx Per Serving: *Cal 139; Prot 10.1 g; Carbo 5.4 g; T Fat 7.8 g; Chol 28.0 mg; Potas 144.0 mg; Sod 427.0 mg.*

Debora S. Wilson
Parker, Colorado

SPICY COCKTAIL MEATBALLS

1 pound lean ground beef
1 envelope dry taco
   seasoning mix
1 egg, beaten
Dash of cayenne pepper
1/8 teaspoon salt
1/8 teaspoon pepper
1 4-ounce can chopped
   green chilies
1/2 cup chopped onion
2 tablespoons margarine
1 tablespoon flour
1/2 cup milk
1/2 cup shredded
   Monterey Jack cheese
1 1/2 cups shredded
   Cheddar cheese
2 tablespoons coarsely
   chopped tomato

Combine ground beef, taco seasoning mix, egg, cayenne pepper, salt and pepper in bowl; mix well. Shape into 1-inch balls; place on rack in broiler pan. Broil until brown on all sides. Sauté chilies and onion in margarine in skillet over medium heat until tender. Add flour; mix well. Stir in milk gradually. Cook until thickened, stirring constantly. Add cheeses. Cook until cheeses are melted, stirring constantly. Stir in tomato. Pour into chafing dish. Add meatballs. Serve hot. Yield: 4 servings.

Approx Per Serving: *Cal 718; Prot 44.3 g; Carbo 27.5 g; T Fat 48.0 g; Chol 217.0 mg; Potas 651.0 mg; Sod 2743.0 mg.*

Linda K. Lervick
Stanwood, Washington

MAKE AHEAD SPICY SNACKS

1 pound pork sausage
1 pound ground chuck
1 pound Velveeta cheese,
   cubed
1 tablespoon oregano
1 tablespoon
   Worcestershire sauce
2 loaves party rye bread

Brown sausage and ground chuck in skillet, stirring until crumbly; drain. Add cheese, oregano and Worcestershire sauce, stirring until cheese melts. Spread on rye bread. Place on baking sheets; freeze until firm. Store in plastic bag in freezer until serving time. Arrange on 10x15-inch baking sheets. Bake at 400 degrees for 10 minutes. Yields: 60 appetizers.

Approx Per Appetizer: *Cal 116; Prot 4.9 g; Carbo 8.1 g; T Fat 7.0 g; Chol 15.1 mg; Potas 88.5 mg; Sod 235.0 mg.*

Judy Fojtik
Ingleside, Illinois

GARLIC BASIL SOUP

This soup is a wonderful warm up for lunch, just before dinner or after touring Heartland Farm on a brisk Dakota morning.

2 tablespoons olive oil
5 cloves of garlic, minced
1 large bay leaf
2 tablespoons chopped
   fresh basil
1 teaspoon flour
4 cups hot beef broth
1/8 teaspoon salt
1/8 teaspoon freshly
   ground pepper
1/8 teaspoon Tabasco
   sauce
1/8 teaspoon white pepper
1/4 teaspoon garlic
   powder
2 egg yolks, lightly
   beaten
1 tablespoon minced
   parsley
4 thin slices French
   bread, toasted

Bring olive oil to the smoking point in skillet over medium-high heat. Add garlic and bay leaf. Sauté until garlic is brown, stirring constantly. Add basil. Sauté for 1 minute longer. Add flour. Cook for 3 minutes, stirring constantly. Stir in 1 cup beef broth gradually. Pour into stockpot. Add remaining beef broth. Add salt, pepper, Tabasco sauce, white pepper and garlic powder; mix well. Bring to a low simmer over medium heat. Cook for 10 minutes. Combine 1 cup soup mixture and egg yolks in small bowl; beat well. Pour into soup mixture. Add parsley; stir well. Place French bread in soup bowls. Ladle soup over bread. Serve immediately. Recipe may be prepared up to the point of adding soup mixture to egg yolks. Chill until ready to reheat and continue preparation. Do not store soup in freezer. Yield: 4 servings.

Approx Per Serving: *Cal 225; Prot 6.7 g; Carbo 23.0 g; T Fat 11.7 g; Chol 137.0 mg; Potas 177.0 mg; Sod 1638.0 mg.*

Jayne D. Solberg, Heartland Farms
Baltic, South Dakota

WILD RICE SOUP

This is a very hearty and delicious soup that is almost hearty enough for
a casserole. This recipe came from the Indian reservation.

1 cup uncooked wild rice
1 pound bacon
1 onion, chopped
2 cups half and half
2 4-ounce cans
   mushrooms, undrained
2 cans cream of potato
   soup
16 ounces Old English
   cheese

Soak wild rice in water to cover in large saucepan overnight. Cook in water to cover until tender. Brown bacon in skillet; remove; drain on paper towels and crumble. Sauté onion in bacon drippings in skillet until tender; drain. Combine bacon, onion, half and half, mushrooms, soup and wild rice in soup kettle. Add cheese. Cook until cheese is melted and soup is heated to serving temperature, stirring constantly. Do not scorch. Yield: 8 servings.

Approx Per Serving: *Cal 697; Prot 34.4 g; Carbo 18.4 g; T Fat 54.2 g; Chol 128.0 mg; Potas 610.0 mg; Sod 2468.0 mg.*

Patricia Trapp
Big Bend, Wisconsin

ZUCCHINI SOUP

This is our favorite winter soup. I freeze the zucchini mixture in 1-quart jars
when our garden is producing and make soup all winter.

6 cups chopped
   unpeeled zucchini
1 cup water
2 tablespoons instant
   minced onion
2 teaspoons seasoned salt
1 teaspoon parsley flakes
4 teaspoons instant
   chicken bouillon
¼ cup butter
¼ cup flour
¼ teaspoon white pepper
2 cups milk
1 cup light cream

Combine zucchini, water, onion, seasoned salt, parsley flakes and bouillon in large saucepan. Cook until zucchini is tender, stirring frequently. Pour into blender container. Process until puréed. Melt butter in large saucepan. Add flour; stir until smooth. Add zucchini mixture, white pepper, milk and cream. Heat to serving temperature, stirring frequently. Garnish with dollop of sour cream or croutons. May be served cold. Zucchini purée may be frozen and soup preparation completed at a later time. Yield: 8 servings.

Approx Per Serving: *Cal 209; Prot 4.5 g; Carbo 11.0 g; T Fat 17.2 g; Chol 56.9 mg; Potas 386.0 mg; Sod 693.0 mg.*

Martha Haven
Grand Junction, Colorado

The Watering Hole

FILLIES DELIGHT

4 ounces dark Cacao
4 ounces Brandy
4 ounces peppermint
schnapps
3 cups hot chocolate
1 cup whipped cream

Combine Cacao, Brandy and schnapps in container; mix well. Pour into prepared hot chocolate; mix well. Ladle into mugs. Top with dollops of whipped cream. Yield: 2 servings.

Nutritional information is not available.

Cecile K. Hetzel Dunn
Temecula, California

FROZEN BANANA PUNCH

1 12-ounce can frozen
  orange juice
  concentrate, thawed
4 cups sugar
6 cups water
5 bananas, mashed
Juice of 2 lemons
1 46-ounce can
  pineapple juice
3 28-ounce bottles of
  ginger ale, chilled

Prepare orange juice using package directions. Heat sugar and water in large saucepan over medium heat, stirring until sugar is dissolved; remove from heat. Let stand for several minutes. Add orange juice, bananas, lemon juice and pineapple juice; mix well. Pour into freezer containers. Seal tightly. Freeze until firm. Remove from freezer 6 hours before serving. Place in large punch bowl. Stir in ginger ale gradually. Banana mixture may be stored in freezer for several months. Yield: 50 servings.

Approx Per Serving: *Cal 114; Prot 0.4 g; Carbo 29.1 g; T Fat 0.1 g; Chol 0.0 mg; Potas 130.0 mg; Sod 4.3 mg.*

Marilynn Hajek
Longmont, Colorado

OASIS PUNCH

This punch was served at the Indiana Arabian Horse Club parties.

1 8-ounce can frozen
  lemonade concentrate,
  thawed
1 cup orange juice
1 envelope unsweetened
  cherry drink mix
1 envelope unsweetened
  strawberry drink mix
2 cups sugar
8 cups water
1 to 2 liters ginger ale,
  chilled

Combine lemonade concentrate, orange juice, drink mixes, sugar and water in large container, stirring until sugar and drink mixes are dissolved. Let stand for 2 hours. Pour into punch bowl. Stir in ginger ale. Yield: 40 servings.

Approx Per Serving: *Cal 59; Prot 0.1 g; Carbo 15.2 g; T Fat 0.0 g; Chol 0.0 mg; Potas 16.9 mg; Sod 2.1 mg.*

Marjorie Day
Ocala, Florida

PINK PUNCH

1 12-ounce can frozen lemonade concentrate, thawed
2 quarts cranberry juice, chilled
2 quarts ginger ale, chilled
1 pint raspberry sherbet

Combine lemonade concentrate, cranberry juice and ginger ale in punch bowl; mix well. Float scoops of sherbet on top. Yield: 25 servings.

Approx Per Serving: *Cal 123; Prot 0.3 g; Carbo 30.2 g; T Fat 0.4 g; Chol 1.3 mg; Potas 43.3 mg; Sod 15.7 mg.*

Marilynn Hajek
Longmont, Colorado

WHITE WINE SANGRIA

3 cups white wine
1/2 cup Triple Sec
1/4 cup sugar
1 orange, sliced
1 lime, sliced
1 10-ounce bottle of club soda, chilled

Combine wine, Triple Sec and sugar in glass container; stir until sugar is dissolved. Add fruit. Chill, covered, for 1 hour. Add soda and ice; stir gently. Pour into pitcher. Yield: 6 servings.

Approx Per Serving: *Cal 207; Prot 0.4 g; Carbo 22.0 g; T Fat 0.1 g; Chol 0.0 mg; Potas 125.0 mg; Sod 16.7 mg.*

Marion Gardner
Waco, Texas

PEACHY VANILLA SHAKE

Excellent for people on diets. Wonderful summer drink.

1 cup ice water
2 envelopes Alba vanilla shake mix
6 ice cubes
1 peach, peeled, chopped
Dash of nutmeg

Combine water and shake mix in blender container. Add ice cubes 1 at a time, processing at low speed constantly. Process at high speed for 60 seconds or until mixture is thickened and ice cubes are completely crushed. Add peach and nutmeg; process until smooth. Yield: 2 servings.

Approx Per Serving: *Cal 19; Prot 0.3 g; Carbo 4.9 g; T Fat 0.1 g; Chol 0.0 mg; Potas 86.0 mg; Sod 0.0 mg.*
Nutritional information does not include Alba vanilla shake mix.

Cecile K. Hetzel Dunn
Temecula, California

FRIENDSHIP TEA

2 cups Tang
2 cups sugar
1 envelope lemonade
  drink mix
1½ teaspoons cinnamon
1 cup instant tea mix

Combine Tang, sugar, lemonade mix, cinnamon and instant tea mix in bowl; mix well. Store in tightly covered container. Place 2 to 3 teaspoons tea mixture in 1 cup hot water; stir well. Yield: 96 tablespoons.

Nutritional information is not available.

Nell B. and W. C. "Dub" Miller
Dallas, Texas

ARABIAN COFFEE (Qahwa Arabeya)

3 cups water
¾ of an-Arab-coffee-cup
  of Arab coffee
1 Arab-coffee-cup of
  cardamom, coarsely
  ground
¼ teaspoon saffron

Bring water to a boil in saucepan. Add coffee; stir well. Boil for 30 minutes over low heat. Remove from heat. Let stand for 5 minutes. Place cardamom in large pot. Strain coffee into pot. Add saffron. Bring to a boil; remove from heat. Yield: 6 servings.

Nutritional information is not available.

*Excerpted from **Aramco World***

ARABIAN MINT TEA

Green China tea
2 to 3 teaspoons sugar
Fresh dark-green mint
  leaves without stalks,
  crushed

Place heaping spoonful of tea in good-sized warmed teapot. Add a small amount of boiling water, sugar to taste and crushed mint leaves, pushing mint leaves to bottom of teapot. Fill teapot with boiling water. Steep tea for a moment or two before drinking.

Nutritional information is not available.

*Excerpted from **Aramco World***

Green Greens

Salads

LONI'S CAESAR SALAD

Exercise and rabbit food will help you to look like the lovely Loni Anderson.

Mixed salad greens
1 clove of garlic, crushed
1/4 cup olive oil
1 teaspoon
  Worcestershire sauce
1/4 teaspoon freshly
  ground pepper
2 anchovies, mashed
1 egg, coddled
1/4 cup lemon juice
1/2 cup Parmesan cheese
2 cups croutons

Tear salad greens, such as romaine, leaf lettuce, iceberg lettuce and watercress into salad bowl. Combine garlic and oil in bowl; mix well. Add Worcestershire sauce, pepper and anchovies; mix well. Add coddled egg in the oil and garlic mixture; mix well. Pour over greens. Toss until well coated. Sprinkle with lemon juice and cheese; toss lighty. Top with croutons. Serve immediately. Yield: 6 servings.

Approx Per Serving: *Cal 214; Prot 12.9 g; Carbo 8.6 g; T Fat 14.2 g; Chol 77.0 mg; Potas 200.0 mg; Sod 320.0 mg.*
Nutritional information does not include salad greens.

Loni Anderson
Jupiter, Florida

ORANGE AND FENNEL SALAD

4 large navel oranges
1 head fennel
1/2 cup olive oil
1/4 cup (or more)
  imported black Italian
  olives
Spinach leaves

Peel and section oranges over bowl to retain juice. Place oranges in bowl with juice. Discard outer fennel leaves. Slice remaining leaves thinly crosswise. Add to oranges; toss lightly. Drizzle olive oil over salad. Sprinkle with salt and pepper to taste. Add olives; toss. Marinate for 30 minutes. Spoon onto spinach-lined plates. Yield: 4 servings.

Approx Per Serving: *Cal 322; Prot 1.4 g; Carbo 15.8 g; T Fat 30.3 g; Chol 0.0 mg; Potas 240.0 mg; Sod 107.0 mg.*

Paolo Gucci
New York, New York

GREEN HORSE SHOW GORK

This salad is great anytime; it's light, but filling. I learned the basic recipe many years ago while working in a delicatessen and have modified it to my tastes.

1   3-ounce package lime
    gelatin
1   8-ounce can crushed
    pineapple
1¼ cups miniature
    marshmallows
2 cups small curd cottage
    cheese
8 ounces whipped
    topping

Make gelatin according to package directions for quick-set method using 7 ice cubes. Drain pineapple, reserving juice. Combine reserved juice and marshmallows in saucepan. Cook over low heat until marshmallows are almost melted, stirring frequently. Add to gelatin; mix well. Add cottage cheese and pineapple; mix well. Chill in refrigerator until partially set. Fold in whipped topping. Pour into containers for travelling. Chill until firm. Do not cover tightly after serving or salad will become watery. Gelatin can be chilled in freezer for 30 minutes for faster setting. Yield: 8 servings.

Approx Per Serving: *Cal 281; Prot 9.4 g; Carbo 49.9 g; T Fat 5.8 g; Chol 10.6 mg; Potas 119.0 mg; Sod 297.0 mg.*

Kathy Norton
Yakima, Washington

FRUIT SALAD

This fruit salad is served at the Old Salem Methodist Campground "camp meetings" down on the Mississippi Gulf Coast.

1   15-ounce can
    pineapple chunks
1   16-ounce can sweet
    cherries, drained
1   14-ounce can
    sweetened condensed
    milk
2 cups whipped topping
½ cup chopped pecans

Combine pineapple, cherries, sweetened condensed milk and whipped topping in bowl; mix well. Add pecans; mix well. Chill, covered, in refrigerator overnight. Yield: 8 servings.

Approx Per Serving: *Cal 335; Prot 5.8 g; Carbo 54.4 g; T Fat 12.0 g; Chol 18.9 mg; Potas 381.0 mg; Sod 78.6 mg.*

Deirdre Janney, Ph.D.
Lucedale, Mississippi

POTLUCK FRUIT SALAD

1 16-ounce can fruit
   cocktail
1 15-ounce can
   pineapple chunks
1 3-ounce package
   vanilla pudding and
   pie filling mix
1 11-ounce can
   mandarin oranges,
   drained
Mixed fresh fruit in
   season

Drain fruit cocktail and pineapple, reserving juices. Add enough water to reserved juices to measure 1½ cups. Cook pudding mix according to package directions using juice mixture. Cool. Combine fruit cocktail, pineapple chunks, mandarin oranges and fresh fruit in bowl. Add pudding mixture; toss lightly. Chill until serving time. Strawberries, blueberries, bananas, peaches and any melon except watermelon are good additions.
Yield: 6 servings.

Approx Per Serving: *Cal 195; Prot 0.8 g; Carbo 50.4 g; T Fat 0.2 g; Chol 0.0 mg; Potas 181.0 mg; Sod 103.0 mg.*
Nutritional information does not include fresh fruit.

Barbara L. Mulder
Hastings, Michigan

RASPBERRY SUPREME SALAD

1 5-ounce package
   raspberry gelatin
½ cup sugar
1 16-ounce can
   raspberries
1 8-ounce can juice-
   pack crushed
   pineapple
8 ounces cream cheese,
   softened
1 cup sour cream
½ cup chopped walnuts
1 teaspoon vanilla extract

Combine gelatin, sugar, raspberries and pineapple in saucepan. Bring to a boil, stirring constantly. Cook until gelatin and sugar are dissolved, stirring constantly. Pour into mold. Chill until partially set. Combine cream cheese, sour cream, walnuts and vanilla in mixer bowl. Beat until mixed well. Pour into mold. Chill until set. Unmold onto serving plate.
Yield: 10 servings.

Approx Per Serving: *Cal 313; Prot 5.1 g; Carbo 39.3 g; T Fat 16.5 g; Chol 35.0 mg; Potas 161.0 mg; Sod 127.0 mg.*

Dana C. Ham
Winnemucca, Nevada

HOLIDAY STRAWBERRY SALAD

2½ cups crushed pretzels
3 tablespoons brown
  sugar
¾ cup melted butter
8 ounces cream cheese,
  softened
1 egg
1 cup confectioners' sugar
¼ teaspoon lemon extract
2 3-ounce packages
  strawberry gelatin
2 cups boiling water
2 10-ounce packages
  frozen strawberries

Combine crushed pretzels, brown sugar and butter in bowl; mix well. Press over bottom and sides of 9x13-inch dish. Beat cream cheese, egg, confectioners' sugar and lemon extract in mixer bowl until smooth. Spread over crust. Chill in refrigerator until set. Dissolve gelatin in boiling water in bowl. Add strawberries. Chill until partially set. Pour over cream cheese layer. Chill until set. Cut into squares. Yield: 12 servings.

Approx Per Serving: Cal 446; Prot 8.0 g; Carbo 66.7 g; T Fat 20.3 g; Chol 74.5 mg; Potas 161.0 mg; Sod 962.0 mg.

Mary Jane Parkinson
El Cajon, California

STRAWBERRY SOUR CREAM SALAD

My mom (Betty) makes this stuff. In my book it ranks right up there with pinto beans and corn bread.

2 3-ounce packages
  strawberry gelatin
2½ cups boiling water
1 10-ounce package
  frozen strawberries
3 bananas, sliced
½ cup chopped pecans
1 cup sour cream

Dissolve gelatin in boiling water in bowl. Add frozen strawberries; stir occasionally until berries are thawed. Add bananas and pecans; mix well. Pour half the mixture into 8x8-inch dish. Chill in refrigerator until set. Spread sour cream over layer. Pour remaining gelatin mixture over sour cream. Chill in refrigerator until set. May substitute fresh strawberries for frozen and add sugar if desired. Yield: 6 servings.

Approx Per Serving: Cal 322; Prot 5.4 g; Carbo 46.1 g; T Fat 15.1 g; Chol 17.0 mg; Potas 389.0 mg; Sod 112.0 mg.

Gary L. Carpenter
Longmont, Colorado

CHINESE CHICKEN SALAD

*This is a quick and delicious summer lunch. I recommend it
as a main dish. It can be made ahead and is great for a crowd.*

3 chicken breast filets
2 slices fresh gingerroot
1 head lettuce, torn
3 green onions, chopped
1/2 cup sliced almonds,
  toasted
1/4 cup sesame seed
1 3-ounce can Chinese
  noodles
1/4 cup sugar
1 teaspoon salt
1/2 teaspoon pepper
1/4 cup rice wine vinegar
1/2 cup oil

Combine chicken, gingerroot and water to
cover in saucepan. Bring to a boil; reduce
heat. Cook for 20 minutes. Drain and chop
chicken. Chill in refrigerator. Combine lettuce, onions, almonds, sesame seed and
noodles in salad bowl. Add chicken. Combine sugar, salt, pepper, vinegar and oil in
small bowl. Pour over chicken mixture;
toss lightly. May substitute deep-fried
won ton strips for noodles.
Yield: 4 servings.

Approx Per Serving: *Cal 616; Prot 23.9 g; Carbo 31.1 g; T Fat 46.1 g; Chol 44.2 mg;
    Potas 457.0 mg; Sod 793.0 mg.*

*Barbara McKenzie
Bellevue, Washington*

ENSALADA MUY SABROSA

*This is my version of a salad that my friend and former housekeeper, Rosa Rúiz, and
I came up with. Rosa is from the Mexican state of Oaxaca, and can flat COOK!*

8 chicken breast filets
3 tablespoons peanut oil
1 10-ounce can tomatoes
  and green chilies
2 4-ounce cans chopped
  green chilies
2 cloves of garlic, minced
3 tablespoons dried
  cilantro
2 cups sour cream
12 corn tortillas
Oil for deep frying
2 heads romaine lettuce
2 avocados, peeled,
  chopped

Cut chicken filets into 1-inch pieces. Sauté in
oil in skillet until browned. Add tomatoes,
chilies, garlic and cilantro; mix well. Simmer
for 45 to 60 minutes or until chicken is very
tender. Remove from heat; stir in sour cream.
Let stand, covered, for several minutes. Cut
tortillas into julienne strips. Deep-fry several
at a time until golden; drain on paper towels.
Tear lettuce into bite-sized pieces. Arrange on
serving plates. Spoon chicken mixture onto
lettuce-lined salad plates. Top with avocados
and tortilla strips. This salad is good with
black beans cooked with onions and bacon,
warm corn tortillas and butter and crisp dry
white wine. Yield: 4 servings.

Approx Per Serving: *Cal 1044; Prot 67.9 g; Carbo 62.9 g; T Fat 60.9 g;
    Chol 194.0 mg; Potas 1995.0 mg; Sod 334.0 mg.
    Nutritional information does not include oil for deep frying.*

*Linda White
Nicholasville, Kentucky*

WRIGLEY BUILDING RESTAURANT COBB SALAD

This is an old-time favorite of the Wrigley Building Restaurant in Chicago.

1/2 head iceberg lettuce
1/2 head romaine lettuce
1/2 bunch watercress
1 small bunch chicory
 endive
2 tablespoons minced
 chives
2 medium tomatoes
1 chicken breast filet,
 cooked, chopped
6 slices crisp-fried
 bacon, crumbled
1 avocado, chopped
3 hard-boiled eggs,
 chopped
1/2 cup crumbled
 Roquefort cheese
1/2 cup salad dressing

Combine iceberg and romaine lettuce, watercress and endive in food processor container; process until finely chopped. Place in salad bowl. Add chives. Peel, seed and chop tomatoes. Arrange tomato, chicken, bacon, avocado and eggs in narrow strips or wedges over greens. Sprinkle with cheese. Chill until serving time. Add salad dressing just before serving; toss lightly. Yield: 6 servings.

Approx Per Serving: *Cal 242; Prot 15.4 g; Carbo 6.6 g; T Fat 17.8 g; Chol 172.0 mg; Potas 577.0 mg; Sod 507.0 mg.*
Nutritional information does not include salad dressing.

Julie A. Wrigley, Wrigley Arabians
Lake Geneva, Wisconsin

SHRIMP SALAD

1 1/2 cups cooked broken
 spaghetti
4 hard-boiled eggs,
 chopped
1 8-ounce can English
 peas, drained
1/2 cup chopped green
 bell pepper
1/2 cup chopped celery
3/4 cup chopped black
 olives
1 1/2 cups cooked shrimp
Mayonnaise

Combine spaghetti, eggs, peas, pepper, celery, olives and shrimp in salad bowl; toss gently. Add desired amount of mayonnaise; toss until coated. Serve on lettuce-lined salad plates. May substitute remoulade sauce for mayonnaise. Yield: 6 servings.

Approx Per Serving: *Cal 233; Prot 19.6 g; Carbo 16.5 g; T Fat 10.9 g; Chol 293.0 mg; Potas 285.0 mg; Sod 479.0 mg.*
Nutritional information does not include mayonnaise.

Anita R. Kamperman
Dallas, Texas

SHRIMP SALAD SUPREME

1/2 cup instant rice
1/2 pound cooked
  shrimp, chopped
1/2 cup finely chopped
  green bell pepper
1 cup chopped
  cauliflower
Juice of 1/2 lemon
1/2 cup mayonnaise-type
  salad dressing

Cook rice using package directions. Chill in refrigerator. Combine shrimp, green pepper, cauliflower, lemon juice and salad dressing in bowl; mix well. Add rice; toss gently. Chill until serving time. Yield: 3 servings.

Approx Per Serving: *Cal 304; Prot 18.2 g; Carbo 26.7 g; T Fat 14.1 g; Chol 157.0 mg; Potas 346.0 mg; Sod 453.0 mg.*

Marjorie Day
Ocala, Florida

COLD RICE SALAD

1/2 cup wild rice, cooked,
  chilled
1/2 cup brown rice,
  cooked, chilled
1/2 cup white rice, cooked,
  chilled
1 cup slivered almonds
3 green onions, chopped
4 stalks celery, chopped
1/2 cup chopped
  cucumber
2 navel oranges, peeled,
  chopped
1 teaspoon Dijon mustard
1/2 cup olive oil
1/4 cup red wine vinegar
2 tablespoons
  mayonnaise
1/8 teaspoon sugar

Combine rices in large bowl; mix well. Add almonds, onions, celery, cucumber and oranges; toss lightly. Combine mustard, olive oil, vinegar, mayonnaise, sugar and salt and pepper to taste in small bowl; whisk until well mixed. Pour dressing over salad gradually; toss lightly. Chill, covered, in refrigerator. Bring to room temperature before serving. Yield: 6 servings.

Approx Per Serving: *Cal 410; Prot 6.8 g; Carbo 24.3 g; T Fat 33.7 g; Chol 2.7 mg; Potas 411.0 mg; Sod 64.2 mg.*

Ruth Boyd
Denver, Colorado

COLD CURRIED RICE

1 package chicken-
   flavored Rice-A-Roni
2 jars marinated
   artichoke hearts
12 green olives, thinly
   sliced
4 green onions, thinly
   sliced
1/2 green bell pepper,
   finely chopped
1/3 cup mayonnaise
3/4 teaspoon curry powder

Cook Rice-A-Roni using package directions. Chill in refrigerator. Drain and slice artichoke hearts, reserving marinade. Combine olives, green onions, green pepper, Rice-A-Roni and artichoke hearts in bowl; mix well. Blend reserved marinade, mayonnaise and curry powder in small bowl. Add to salad; toss lightly. Chill in refrigerator for 2 hours or longer. Yield: 4 servings.

Approx Per Serving: *Cal 458; Prot 6.7 g; Carbo 62.5 g; T Fat 21.1 g; Chol 10.7 mg; Potas 285.0 mg; Sod 689.0 mg.*

Debora S. Wilson
Parker, Colorado

ARABIAN CUCUMBER AND YOGURT SALAD

4 cucumbers
2 cloves of garlic
2 cups plain yogurt
1/4 teaspoon salt
1 tablespoon dried mint

Peel cucumbers. Cut into halves lengthwise; slice thinly. Pound garlic with mortar and pestle. Mix with yogurt and salt in bowl. Add cucumbers. Sprinkle with mint. Chill until serving time. Yield: 4 servings.

Nutritional information is not available.

Excerpted from **Aramco World**

ARABIAN PARSLEY AND CRACKED WHEAT SALAD

1/2 cup bulgur
11/2 cups finely chopped
   parsley
1/2 cup finely chopped
   fresh mint
3 green onions, finely
   chopped
1 large tomato, chopped
6 tablespoons lemon
   juice
1/4 cup olive oil
1 head romaine lettuce

Rinse bulgur in water; drain and squeeze dry. Combine bulgur, parsley, mint, green onions and tomato in bowl; mix well. Add lemon juice, olive oil and salt to taste; mix well. Line salad bowl with lettuce leaves. Spoon mixture into bowl. Use lettuce leaves as edible spoons to scoop out salad. This is the traditional way to eat tabouli; it can, of course, be served on salad plates and eaten with forks. Yield: 6 servings.

Nutritional information is not available.

Excerpted from **Aramco World**

BLUE CHEESE GARDEN SALAD

This is an excellent make-ahead salad for after riding.

1 cup ricotta cheese
3/4 cup mayonnaise
2 tablespoons half and
  half
6 cups torn spinach
  leaves
4 ounces blue cheese,
  crumbled
1 cup sliced carrots
1 cup sliced mushrooms
1/2 red onion, thinly
  sliced
1 1/2 cups cooked peas
2 hard-boiled eggs, sliced
5 slices crisp-fried
  bacon, crumbled

Combine ricotta, mayonnaise and half and half in bowl; mix well. Layer spinach, half the dressing, half the blue cheese and all the carrots, mushrooms, onion, peas and egg slices in large salad bowl. Top with remaining dressing and blue cheese. Sprinkle with bacon. Serve immediately or chill, covered, in refrigerator until serving time. Yield: 6 servings.

Approx Per Serving: *Cal 502; Prot 21.5 g; Carbo 23.0 g; T Fat 38.3 g; Chol 149.0 mg; Potas 911.0 mg; Sod 780.0 mg.*

Debby Cain
Oregon, Illinois

BROCCOLI SALAD

2 10-ounce packages
  frozen chopped broccoli
10 stuffed green olives,
  chopped
4 green onions, chopped
4 hard-boiled eggs,
  chopped
4 stalks celery, chopped
1/2 teaspoon salt
Mayonnaise

Cook broccoli using package directions; drain. Add olives, onions, eggs, celery and salt; mix well. Stir in enough mayonnaise to moisten as desired. Chill in refrigerator until serving time. Use fewer olives for low calorie or low sodium dish. May substitute fresh broccoli for frozen. Yield: 4 servings.

Approx Per Serving: *Cal 336; Prot 11.4 g; Carbo 11.2 g; T Fat 29.2 g; Chol 290.0 mg; Potas 481.0 mg; Sod 795.0 mg.*
Nutritional information does not include mayonnaise.

Debora S. Wilson
Parker, Colorado

CAESAR SALAD FOR TWO

8 teaspoons olive oil
1 tablespoon red wine
  vinegar
1 teaspoon dry mustard
1 teaspoon (10 drops)
  Worcestershire sauce
1 clove of garlic, crushed
1 teaspoon lemon juice
1 egg yolk
3 anchovies, mashed
Romaine lettuce
20 croutons
1/4 cup Parmesan cheese

Chill two salad plates in freezer. Combine olive oil, vinegar, mustard, Worcestershire sauce, garlic, lemon juice, egg yolk and anchovies in bowl; mix well with fork or wire whisk. Tear desired amount of lettuce into salad bowl. Add dressing; toss to coat. Add croutons, cheese and freshly ground pepper to taste. Serve immediately on chilled salad plates. Yield: 2 servings.

Approx Per Serving: *Cal 571; Prot 31.3 g; Carbo 43.9 g; T Fat 30.2 g; Chol 203.0 mg; Potas 623.0 mg; Sod 1044.0 mg.*
Nutritional information does not include lettuce.

Robert M. Brunson
Beverly Hills, California

LEE'S FAVORITE SALAD

4 slices bacon
1/3 cup catsup
1 teaspoon
  Worcestershire sauce
1 cup oil
1 small onion, chopped
1/4 cup wine vinegar
3/4 cup sugar
2 heads Boston lettuce
2 hard-boiled eggs

Fry bacon in skillet until crisp; drain. Drain on paper towels. Combine catsup, Worcestershire sauce, oil, onion, vinegar, sugar and salt and pepper to taste in small bowl; mix well. Tear lettuce into bite-sized pieces; place in salad bowl. Add eggs; toss lightly. Pour desired amount of dressing over salad; toss lightly. Crumble bacon over top. Yield: 6 servings.

Approx Per Serving: *Cal 505; Prot 4.9 g; Carbo 33.3 g; T Fat 40.6 g; Chol 94.9 mg; Potas 348.0 mg; Sod 260.0 mg.*
Nutritional information includes entire amount of salad dressing.

Mrs. Lee Bossen
Clinton, Iowa

HEARTS OF PALM SALAD

2 tablespoons wine
  vinegar
6 tablespoons oil
1/2 teaspoon salt
1/8 teaspoon pepper
1 head lettuce
2 14-ounce cans hearts
  of palm, drained
2 large avocados

Combine vinegar, oil, salt and pepper in small jar; shake well. Let stand at room temperature for 8 hours or chill overnight. Tear lettuce into bite-sized pieces; place in salad bowl. Chop hearts of palm into 1/4-inch pieces. Place on top of lettuce. Chill, covered, until serving time. Peel and cut avocados into 1/2-inch pieces. Add to salad; toss lightly. Add just enough dressing to moisten; toss lightly. Store any remaining dressing in airtight container in refrigerator for another use.
Yield: 8 servings.

Nutritional information is not available.

Ruth Husband
Brea, California

POTATO SALAD

3/4 to 1 cup mayonnaise
1/4 to 1/2 cup mustard
2 teaspoons parsley
1 teaspoon minced garlic
1/2 to 1 teaspoon salt
1/2 to 1 teaspoon cayenne
  pepper
1/2 teaspoon black pepper
4 potatoes, peeled,
  boiled, chopped
4 hard-boiled eggs,
  chopped

Combine mayonnaise, mustard, parsley, garlic, salt, cayenne and pepper in large bowl; mix well. Fold in potatoes and eggs. Chill until serving time. The dressing can be varied by adding mayonnaise or mustard until of desired flavor and consistency. Final taste should be sweet with a bite.
Yield: 6 servings.

Approx Per Serving: *Cal 339; Prot 6.6 g; Carbo 20.7 g; T Fat 26.2 g; Chol 199.0 mg; Potas 389.0 mg; Sod 516.0 mg.*

Steve and Rebecca Galloway
Lexington, Kentucky

CASHEW SPINACH SALAD

1 cup oil
1/4 cup vinegar
1/3 cup sugar
1 tablespoon celery seed
1 teaspoon dry mustard
1 teaspoon salt
1/4 cup minced onion
Salad greens
3/4 cup cashews
3/4 cup cubed cream
  cheese

Combine oil, vinegar, sugar, celery seed, mustard, salt and onion in small bowl; mix well. Place salad greens in large bowl. Add cashews and cream cheese; toss lightly. Pour dressing over greens; toss lightly. Yield: 6 servings.

Approx Per Serving: *Cal 574; Prot 5.1 g; Carbo 18.9 g; T Fat 55.0 g; Chol 32.6 mg; Potas 169.0 mg; Sod 556.0 mg.*
Nutritional information does not include salad greens.

Jill S. Myles
Fort Collins, Colorado

SPINACH SALAD

1 cup soybean oil
1/2 cup cider vinegar
1 medium onion, finely
  chopped
1/3 cup catsup
3/4 cup sugar
1 tablespoon
  Worcestershire sauce
2 teaspoons salt
1/2 bunch fresh spinach
1/2 head romaine lettuce
4 water chestnuts, thinly
  sliced
4 hard-boiled eggs,
  chopped
1   16-ounce can bean
  sprouts, drained
8 ounces crisp-fried
  bacon, crumbled

Combine oil, vinegar, onion, catsup, sugar, Worcestershire sauce and salt in small bowl; mix well. Tear spinach and lettuce into bite-sized pieces; place in salad bowl. Add water chestnuts, eggs, bean sprouts and bacon; toss lightly. Chill overnight. Pour a small amount of dressing over salad just before serving; toss lightly. Serve remaining dressing on the side. Yield: 4 servings.

Approx Per Serving: *Cal 1104; Prot 27.2 g; Carbo 54.5 g; T Fat 88.4 g; Chol 322.0 mg; Potas 823.0 mg; Sod 2350.0 mg.*

Barbara L. Mulder
Hastings, Michigan

UNFORGETTABLE WILTED LETTUCE

This is my own recipe. I am an organic gardener and I wait all winter for this salad.

4 cups leaf lettuce
2 cups chopped fresh
  spinach
8 ounces bacon, chopped
1/4 cup minced onion
1/4 cup apple cider
  vinegar
2 teaspoons brown sugar
Dash each of pumpkin
  pie spice and garlic
  powder

Place lettuce and spinach in salad bowl. Sauté bacon and onion in skillet until crisp; do not drain. Add vinegar, brown sugar, pumpkin pie spice, garlic powder and salt and pepper to taste; mix well. Cook over medium heat for 10 to 15 minutes or until mixture comes to a boil. Pour hot dressing over lettuce; toss lightly. Serve immediately. Yield: 4 servings.

Approx Per Serving: *Cal 346; Prot 18.1 g; Carbo 5.5 g; T Fat 28.1 g; Chol 47.7 mg; Potas 457.0 mg; Sod 908.0 mg.*

Janet Smith
Oakford, Illinois

MARINATED MIXED VEGETABLE SALAD

1 8-ounce can French-
  style green beans,
  drained
1 8-ounce can petite
  peas, drained
1 8-ounce can Shoe Peg
  corn, drained
1 cup chopped celery
1 cup chopped red onion
1 2-ounce jar chopped
  pimentos
1 green bell pepper,
  chopped
1 cup sugar
3/4 cup vinegar
1/2 cup oil
1 teaspoon salt
1 teaspoon pepper

Combine beans, peas, corn, celery, onion, pimentos and green pepper in bowl; mix well. Combine sugar, vinegar, oil, salt and pepper in saucepan. Bring to a boil. Cool. Pour over vegetables. Chill in refrigerator. May store in refrigerator for several days. Yield: 4 servings.

Approx Per Serving: *Cal 563; Prot 5.6 g; Carbo 79.5 g; T Fat 28.1 g; Chol 0.0 mg; Potas 512.0 mg; Sod 717.0 mg.*

Ruth Husband
Brea, California

JUAN DE SALAD

1 head romaine lettuce
1 cantaloupe, peeled,
    chopped
1/2 purple onion, chopped
1 tomato, chopped
1/4 cup olive oil
1/4 cup wine vinegar

Tear lettuce into bite-sized pieces; place in salad bowl. Add cantaloupe, onion and tomato; toss lightly. Drain well. Sprinkle with salt and pepper to taste. Pour oil and vinegar over salad; toss lightly. Yield: 6 servings.

Approx Per Serving: *Cal 131; Prot 1.9 g; Carbo 11.8 g; T Fat 9.4 g; Chol 0.0 mg; Potas 477.0 mg; Sod 13.3 mg.*

Pamela Arena Weidel, Boxwood Farm
Pennington, New Jersey

HAWAIIAN SALAD

1 small head butter
    lettuce
1 small head red leaf
    lettuce
2   8-ounce cans
    mandarin oranges,
    drained
Mary Jane's Poppy Seed
    Dressing
1 cup coconut
1 cup slivered almonds

Tear lettuce into bite-sized pieces; place in salad bowl. Add oranges and dressing to taste. Top with coconut and almonds. The coconut and almonds may be served separately. Yield: 4 servings.

Approx Per Serving: *Cal 371; Prot 9.2 g; Carbo 36.7 g; T Fat 23.9 g; Chol 0.0 mg; Potas 682.0 mg; Sod 63.3 mg.*
Nutritional information does not include poppy seed dressing.

Mary Lou Walbergh
Malibu, California

STRAWBERRY AND ORANGE POPPY SEED SALAD

1 cup mayonnaise
1 tablespoon poppy seed
1 to 2 teaspoons sugar
1 tablespoon orange juice
1/2 head lettuce, shredded
2 cups sliced strawberries
2 oranges, peeled, sliced

Combine mayonnaise, poppy seed, sugar and orange juice in bowl; mix well. Chill in refrigerator until serving time. Place lettuce in salad bowl. Add strawberries and oranges; toss lightly. Pour dressing over salad; toss to coat. Serve immediately. Yield: 6 servings.

Approx Per Serving: *Cal 312; Prot 1.6 g; Carbo 11.4 g; T Fat 30.1 g; Chol 21.7 mg; Potas 238.0 mg; Sod 210.0 mg.*

Debby Cain
Oregon, Illinois

NICHOLAS'S CAESAR DRESSING

This dressing is best with a salad of romaine lettuce garnished with freshly grated Parmesan cheese and croutons. Most of the ingredients can be varied according to taste.

1 can anchovies
1 cup light olive oil
1 egg
1 teaspoon dry mustard
1/2 cup sherry vinegar
Garlic, Worcestershire
 sauce and Tabasco
 sauce to taste

Combine anchovies, oil, egg, mustard and vinegar in blender container; process until smooth. Add garlic, Worcestershire sauce and Tabasco sauce; mix well. Store in airtight container in refrigerator. Yield: 32 tablespoons.

Approx Per Tablespoon: *Cal 67; Prot 0.9 g; Carbo 0.2 g; T Fat 7.1 g; Chol 11.0 mg; Potas 19.4 mg; Sod 5.9 mg.*

Crete B. Harvey
Stanwood, Washington

MOTHER'S ROQUEFORT CREAM DRESSING

3 tablespoons anchovy
 paste
1 cup sour cream
2 cups mayonnaise
1 clove of garlic, minced
1/2 cup vinegar
2 tablespoons lemon
 juice
1/2 cup chopped parsley
1/3 cup chopped green
 onions
8 ounces blue cheese,
 crumbled

Combine anchovy paste, sour cream, mayonnaise and garlic in bowl; mix well. Add vinegar and lemon juice; mix well. Add parsley, green onions, blue cheese and salt and pepper to taste; mix well. Store in airtight container in refrigerator. Yield: 80 tablespoons.

Approx Per Tablespoon: *Cal 57; Prot 0.9 g; Carbo 0.5 g; T Fat 5.8 g; Chol 7.0 mg; Potas 20.5 mg; Sod 73.1 mg.*

Crete B. Harvey
Stanwood, Washington

The Classic Mane Dishes

Main Dishes

Stable Staples

BURT'S BEEF STEW

I make this stew for Loni and our new son, Quinton Anderson Reynolds.

4 slices bacon, chopped
2½ pounds lean beef
    chuck
¼ cup flour
¼ teaspoon pepper
2 onions, chopped
4 cloves of garlic, minced
1   28-ounce can tomato
    sauce
2 cups dry red wine
4 carrots
4 large potatoes
2 stalks celery, chopped
10 mushrooms, sliced

Cook bacon in heavy saucepan just until light brown. Cut beef into chunks. Coat beef with mixture of flour and pepper. Brown in bacon drippings in saucepan, turning frequently. Add onions and garlic. Cook until light brown. Add tomato sauce and wine. Simmer, covered, for 1½ hours. Chop carrots and potatoes coarsely. Add carrots, potatoes, celery and mushrooms. Simmer, covered, for 30 minutes or until vegetables are tender. Yield: 5 servings.

Approx Per Serving: *Cal 605; Prot 41.1 g; Carbo 53.1 g; T Fat 19.4 g; Chol 115.0 mg; Potas 1828.0 mg; Sod 1162.0 mg.*

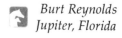
Burt Reynolds
Jupiter, Florida

STUFFED GREEN PEPPERS

I like food, men and horses, though not necessarily in that order. This dish can be made on top of the stove or in the oven.

6 green bell peppers
1 pound ground pork
1/2 cup rice
2 eggs
1/4 cup chopped onion
3 tablespoons chopped
   parsley
2 to 3 cups water
1 tablespoon flour
1 tablespoon oil
2 8-ounce cans tomato
   paste
1 to 2 cups water

Cut off pepper tops and discard seed and membrane. Combine pork, rice, eggs, onion, parsley and salt to taste in bowl; mix well. Stuff into peppers. Place in saucepan or baking pan. Add 2 to 3 cups water. Simmer on stove top or bake at 350 degrees for 30 minutes. Mix flour, oil, tomato paste and sugar and salt to taste in saucepan. Stir in 1 to 2 cups water or enough to make of desired consistency. Simmer until thickened and smooth, stirring constantly. Pour over peppers. Cook for 15 minutes longer or until peppers are tender and pork is cooked through. Yield: 6 servings.

Approx Per Serving: *Cal 406; Prot 22.4 g; Carbo 33.8 g; T Fat 21.2 g; Chol 150.0 mg; Potas 1154.0 mg; Sod 114.0 mg.*

Zsa Zsa Gabor
Los Angeles, California

SAUSAGES WITH PEPPERS AND ONIONS

I love this dish and I wouldn't get married to my lovely wife, Gina, until she learned to make this in her sleep.

1¹/2 pounds sweet or hot
   Italian sausages
2 tablespoons olive oil
3 large onions, slivered
4 cloves of garlic, minced
3 red bell peppers
3 green bell peppers
3 yellow bell peppers
1/2 teaspoon oregano
1/2 teaspoon Italian
   parsley

Brown sausages in 1 tablespoon olive oil in skillet over medium-low heat. Add remaining tablespoon oil, onions and garlic. Sauté until onion is tender. Slice peppers into strips. Stir peppers, oregano and parsley into skillet. Cook until peppers are tender. Yield: 6 servings.

Approx Per Serving: *Cal 277; Prot 13.0 g; Carbo 15.4 g; T Fat 19.0 g; Chol 41.1 mg; Potas 590.0 mg; Sod 496.0 mg.*

Peter DeLuise
of 21 Jump Street
Pacific Palisades, California

MOTHER'S ROAST BEEF

Try this only in an electric oven. The roast will be brown on the outside and be rare inside regardless of the size of the roast. You should start about 10:00 in the morning; be sure not to open the oven door after you put the roast in.

1 4-pound standing rib roast
1 teaspoon seasoning salt

Rub roast with seasoning salt and salt and pepper to taste. Let stand for several minutes. Place rib side up in roasting pan. Roast at 375 degrees for 1 hour. Turn off oven. Leave roast in oven for 6 hours; do not open oven door. Set oven temperature at 375 degrees. Roast for 45 minutes longer. Yield: 8 servings.

Approx Per Serving: *Cal 631; Prot 36.2 g; Carbo 0.0 g; T Fat 52.8 g; Chol 140.0 mg; Potas 487.0 mg; Sod 372.0 mg.*

Barbara Pietruszka
Grand Blanc, Michigan

RITA'S BRISKET

This favorite recipe came from my friend Rita.

4 large onions, sliced
1 4-pound beef brisket
1 clove of garlic, minced
3/4 cup catsup
1 1/4 cups water
1 slice rye bread, torn
1 bay leaf

Place onions in roasting pan. Place brisket on onions. Sprinkle with garlic and salt and pepper to taste. Pour mixture of catsup and water over top. Place bread pieces around brisket. Add bay leaf. Roast at 325 degrees for several hours or until tender. Slice brisket. Combine sliced brisket with cooking liquids in shallow dish; discard bay leaf. Chill for 24 hours. Reheat before serving. Yield: 12 servings.

Approx Per Serving: *Cal 306; Prot 31.3 g; Carbo 9.3 g; T Fat 15.3 g; Chol 96.5 mg; Potas 445.0 mg; Sod 245.0 mg.*

Gail Cohan, Dynasty Arabians II, Inc.
Delray Beach, Florida

TEXAS BRISKET

This brisket recipe came from a good friend in Dallas.

1   2-pound beef brisket
1 medium onion, sliced
3 carrots, sliced
3 stalks celery, sliced
1 bay leaf
1 cup catsup
1/2 cup Worcestershire
  sauce
Tabasco sauce to taste
2 cups water
Several drops of liquid
  smoke
1 teaspoon chili powder

Combine brisket with onion, carrots, celery, bay leaf and cold water to cover in large saucepan. Simmer for 2 hours. Remove brisket to roasting pan, reserving stock for another use. Combine catsup, Worcestershire sauce, Tabasco sauce, 2 cups water, liquid smoke, chili powder and salt and pepper to taste in bowl; mix well. Pour over brisket. Bake at 350 degrees for 1 1/2 hours, adding a small amount of reserved stock if necessary. Discard bay leaf. Slice brisket across the grain. Serve with sauce. Yield: 6 servings.

Approx Per Serving: *Cal 358; Prot 32.3 g; Carbo 21.7 g; T Fat 15.4 g; Chol 96.5 mg; Potas 844.0 mg; Sod 756.0 mg.*

Vivian Blomquist
Sylmar, California

BOB'S LEMON BUTTER STEAK WITH BRANDY SAUCE

The girls at my house always love it when Daddy sets fire to the steak!

1   1 1/2-pound sirloin
  steak
1/2 teaspoon seasoned salt
1/4 teaspoon pepper
1 teaspoon oregano
1/4 cup butter
2 tablespoons lemon
  juice
1/2 teaspoon hot sauce
2 tablespoons
  Worcestershire sauce
1/2 cup apricot Brandy,
  heated

Sprinkle both sides of steak with seasoned salt, pepper and oregano. Heat butter, lemon juice and hot sauce in skillet. Add steak. Cook over high heat until brown on both sides. Reduce heat to medium. Cook for 1 to 2 minutes on each side or almost to desired degree of doneness. Pour Worcestershire sauce and heated Brandy over steak. Ignite sauce; let flames die down. Remove to serving platter. Garnish with lemon slices and parsley. Serve with a crisp salad and bread. Yield: 2 servings.

Approx Per Serving: *Cal 994; Prot 59.2 g; Carbo 25.4 g; T Fat 65.8 g; Chol 241.0 mg; Potas 959.0 mg; Sod 1026.0 mg.*

Bob and Judy Harvey
Lake Geneva, Wisconsin

TOURNEDOS OF BEEF

Serve this with salad, an excellent wine and dessert for special occasions. It is sure to please and impress.

8 ounces mushrooms, sliced
1 tablespoon oil
1 tablespoon butter
2 green onions, sliced
4 thick slices French bread
1 tablespoon oil
2 tablespoons butter
2 cups beef stock
1 tablespoon tomato paste
2 teaspoons (about) cornstarch
2 tablespoons Madeira
1 tablespoon chopped fresh parsley
4 thick filets mignon

Sauté mushrooms in 1 tablespoon oil and 1 tablespoon butter in skillet for 5 minutes. Add green onions and salt and pepper to taste. Cook for 1 minute; set aside. Trim crusts from bread. Brown bread lightly on both sides in 1 tablespoon oil and 2 tablespoons butter in small skillet. Remove from skillet; keep warm. Bring beef stock and tomato paste to a boil in skillet. Blend in cornstarch with wire whisk. Stir in wine. Cook for 1 minute. Stir in mushrooms and parsley. Place steaks on rack in broiler pan. Broil to desired degree of doneness. Place toasted bread on serving plates. Top with steaks. Spoon sauce over steaks. Yield: 4 servings.

Approx Per Serving: Cal 591; Prot 35.4 g; Carbo 23.6 g; T Fat 38.8 g; Chol 121.0 mg; Potas 751.0 mg; Sod 1030.0 mg.

Roberta Ashmore, Rubaiyat Arabians
Loomis, California

BEEF BOURGANAISE

This recipe never lets me down when I need to make a good impression.

3 pounds beef chuck, cubed
1/4 cup shortening
3 tablespoons flour
1/2 teaspoon thyme
1 1/2 teaspoons salt
1/2 teaspoon pepper
1   12-ounce can beef broth
1 cup dry red wine
1   16-ounce can small onions
8 ounces fresh mushrooms

Brown beef in shortening in skillet. Stir in flour, thyme, salt and pepper. Spoon into 2-quart casserole. Pour broth and wine over beef. Bake, covered, at 325 degrees for 2 hours. Add onions and mushrooms. Bake for 1 to 1 1/2 hours longer or until tender. Skim pan juices. Serve over potatoes or rice. Yield: 6 servings.

Approx Per Serving: Cal 722; Prot 40.1 g; Carbo 8.9 g; T Fat 54.8 g; Chol 155.0 mg; Potas 496.0 mg; Sod 820.0 mg.

Marian Studer
Lexington, Kentucky

BOEUF BOURGUIGNON

6 slices bacon
3 pounds lean beef, cubed
1 large carrot, sliced
1 large onion, sliced
1/4 cup flour
1 pound small whole
    onions
1 bay leaf
2 12-ounce cans beef
    broth
1 1/2 cups dry red wine
1 tablespoon tomato paste
2 cloves of garlic, minced
1/4 teaspoon thyme
1 teaspoon salt
1/4 teaspoon pepper
1/4 cup flour
1/2 cup water
1 pound fresh mushrooms
2 tablespoons butter

Cook bacon in skillet until crisp. Remove and crumble bacon. Brown beef in bacon drippings in skillet. Remove beef to drain. Sauté carrot and sliced onion in drippings in skillet. Place carrot and onion in Crock•Pot. Stir in 1/4 cup flour. Add beef, bacon, whole onions and bay leaf. Mix broth, wine, tomato paste, garlic, thyme, salt and pepper in small bowl. Add to Crock•Pot; mix well. Blend 1/4 cup flour with water in cup. Stir into beef mixture. Cook on Low for 4 to 6 hours or until tender. Slice mushrooms. Sauté in butter in skillet. Add to Bourguignon just before serving. Discard bay leaf. Yield: 8 servings.

Approx Per Serving: *Cal 508; Prot 36.9 g; Carbo 16.3 g; T Fat 29.9 g; Chol 123.0 mg; Potas 862.0 mg; Sod 755.0 mg.*

Dorothy Stream, Greengate Farms
San Luis Obispo, California

BEEF STROGANOFF

You may add two chopped cooked chicken breast filets for variety if you like.

1 1/2 pounds tenderized
    round steak
1/2 cup flour
2 tablespoons oil
1 small onion, chopped
8 large mushrooms
1/4 teaspoon garlic powder
2 cans cream of
    mushroom soup
1/2 soup can milk
1 cup sour cream
1 16-ounce package egg
    noodles, cooked

Cut steak into bite-sized pieces. Coat with flour. Brown on all sides in oil in skillet. Add onion, mushrooms and garlic powder. Sauté until onions are tender. Remove with slotted spoon to drain on paper towel. Mix soup and milk in skillet. Cook until heated through. Add steak mixture. Heat to serving temperature. Stir in sour cream just before serving. Serve over noodles. Yield: 6 servings.

Approx Per Serving: *Cal 765; Prot 33.4 g; Carbo 70.5 g; T Fat 37.7 g; Chol 151.0 mg; Potas 607.0 mg; Sod 905.0 mg.*

Debora S. Wilson
Parker, Colorado

MADRAS BEEF CURRY

This dish is served often in regimental messes of the British Army. I had it for Sunday brunch at the British Officers' Club in Berlin.

1 large onion, chopped
1/4 cup oil
1 1/2 pounds beef flank
  steak, cubed
1 tablespoon flour
2 tablespoons (about)
  curry powder
1/2 cup beef stock
1 cup yogurt
1 tablespoon chutney
2 tablespoons tomato
  purée
1 12-ounce can tomatoes
1/2 teaspoon salt

Sauté onion in oil in saucepan. Add beef. Cook until brown on all sides. Stir in flour and curry powder. Cook for 2 minutes. Stir in beef stock, yogurt, chutney, tomato purée, tomatoes and salt. Bring to a boil, stirring constantly; reduce heat. Simmer, covered, for 1 to 2 hours or until tender, stirring occasionally. Serve with rice and toppings such as chutney, raisins, coconut or peanuts. Yield: 4 servings.

Approx Per Serving: *Cal 574; Prot 37.2 g; Carbo 15.7 g; T Fat 40.4 g; Chol 115.0 mg; Potas 925.0 mg; Sod 753.0 mg.*

Lori Grumet
Littleton, Colorado

DUMP STEW

The beef in this easy stew does not have to be browned first.

3 pounds stew beef
6 cups sliced carrots
3 onions, sliced
1 cup chopped celery
1 14-ounce can stewed
  tomatoes
3 large potatoes, chopped
1 tablespoon Beau
  Monde seasoning
1 tablespoon seasoned salt
1 tablespoon salt
1/2 teaspoon pepper
1 tablespoon garlic powder
1 tablespoon sugar
1 tablespoon
  Worcestershire sauce

Combine beef, carrots, onions, celery, tomatoes, potatoes, Beau Monde seasoning, seasoned salt, salt, pepper, garlic powder, sugar and Worcestershire sauce in 2-quart baking dish; mix well. Bake at 275 degrees for 5 hours. Yield: 8 servings.

Approx Per Serving: *Cal 437; Prot 34.0 g; Carbo 35.3 g; T Fat 17.9 g; Chol 93.4 mg; Potas 1188.0 mg; Sod 1789.0 mg.*

Grant and Joyce Johnson
Fargo, North Dakota

VEAL CHOPS WITH BACON AND SHALLOTS

1/4 cup unsalted butter
4 ounces slab bacon,
   trimmed
4 12-ounce 1 1/2-inch
   thick veal loin chops
1/4 cup flour
24 small shallots
2 cups dry red wine
1 cup heavy cream

Heat butter in large skillet until very hot. Chop bacon into 1/4-inch cubes. Sauté in butter over medium heat for 10 minutes or until crisp. Remove and drain bacon on paper towel. Season veal with salt and freshly ground pepper to taste. Coat lightly with flour. Brown in pan drippings over medium heat for 5 minutes. Arrange in single layer in shallow baking dish. Sauté shallots in drippings in skillet for 10 minutes or until golden brown and tender. Remove with slotted spoon to drain. Drain skillet. Add wine. Bring to a boil over high heat, stirring to deglaze skillet. Simmer for 10 minutes or until wine is reduced by half. Stir in cream. Cook for 3 minutes or just until thick enough to coat spoon. Pour over chops. Sprinkle with shallots and bacon. Bake, loosely covered with foil, at 375 degrees for 20 minutes. Serve immediately. Yield: 4 servings.

Approx Per Serving: *Cal 1051; Prot 95.7 g; Carbo 11.2 g; T Fat 59.0 g; Chol 486.0 mg; Potas 1508.0 mg; Sod 700.0 mg.*

Robert M. Brunson
Beverly Hills, California

BEAN BURGER

This family recipe is always served on hunting and camping trips. I make it ahead of time and reheat it for a quick and easy dinner.

2 pounds lean ground
   beef
1 large onion, chopped
3 16-ounce cans dark
   kidney beans
2 cans tomato soup
2 4-ounce cans (or less)
   chopped green chilies
1 7-ounce can green
   chili salsa
2 stalks celery, chopped

Brown ground beef with onion in large skillet, stirring until ground beef is crumbly; drain well. Add garlic salt and pepper to taste. Add undrained beans, soup, green chilies, salsa and celery; mix well. Simmer for 45 minutes or until celery is tender. Serve with hot sauce. Yield: 6 servings.

Approx Per Serving: *Cal 601; Prot 42.9 g; Carbo 54.8 g; T Fat 24.6 g; Chol 98.7 mg; Potas 1408.0 mg; Sod 1629.0 mg.*

Glory Vermilyea
Grand Junction, Colorado

CINDY REUNER'S DENVER CHILI

6 slices bacon, chopped
1 pound ground beef
1 onion, chopped
1 green bell pepper, chopped
2 cloves of garlic, chopped
1 pound Italian sausage
1 cup red wine
1 quart tomatoes
1 16-ounce can kidney beans
1 16-ounce can garbanzo beans
1 teaspoon Worcestershire sauce
1 teaspoon dry mustard
1½ teaspoons chili powder
1 teaspoon celery seed
½ teaspoon salt
1½ teaspoons pepper

Fry bacon in saucepan until crisp. Add ground beef. Cook until brown and crumbly, stirring occasionally. Add onion, green pepper and garlic. Sauté until tender. Cut sausage into ¼-inch pieces. Add sausage, wine, tomatoes, undrained beans, Worcestershire sauce, dry mustard, chili powder, celery seed, salt and pepper to saucepan; mix well. Bring to a boil; reduce heat. Simmer for 1 hour. May cook in slow cooker for 8 hours if preferred. Yield: 6 servings.

Approx Per Serving: *Cal 648; Prot 29.7 g; Carbo 23.4 g; T Fat 45.9 g; Chol 106.0 mg; Potas 1030.0 mg; Sod 1362.0 mg.*

Judy A. Cada
Lincoln, Nebraska

MEXICAN CHORIZO SAUSAGE

This is a recipe from Mexico. Serve it as a main dish with beans, salsa and salad.

2 pounds lean ground beef
1 pound ground pork
3 cloves of garlic, minced
1¼ cups chili powder
1½ teaspoons oregano
1 teaspoon cumin
2 teaspoons salt
2 teaspoons pepper
1 cup dry red wine

Combine ground beef, ground pork, garlic, chili powder, oregano, cumin, salt and pepper in bowl. Add wine; mix well. Chill for 3 days. Shape as desired. Brown in skillet for 10 minutes. May mix with fried potatoes and/or scrambled eggs and serve with tortillas. Yield: 10 servings.

Approx Per Serving: *Cal 366; Prot 27.6 g; Carbo 9.4 g; T Fat 23.8 g; Chol 95.0 mg; Potas 645.0 mg; Sod 661.0 mg.*

Barbara Carabeo
McNeal, Arizona

HALFTIME CHILI

1 cup chopped onion
4 pounds ground beef
2 tablespoons butter
1/2 cup chopped celery
1 1/3 cups catsup
1 cup water
1/4 cup lemon juice
2 tablespoons brown sugar
2 1/2 teaspoons
  Worcestershire sauce
2 teaspoons vinegar
1/2 teaspoon dry mustard
1 tablespoon salt
1 48-ounce can tomato
  juice
6 tablespoons chili powder
2 16-ounce cans red
  kidney beans

Cook onion and ground beef in butter in 5-quart saucepan, stirring until ground beef is crumbly; drain. Add celery, catsup, water, lemon juice, brown sugar, Worcestershire sauce, vinegar, dry mustard and salt; mix well. Simmer for 30 minutes. Stir in tomato juice, chili powder and undrained beans. Simmer for 1 to 2 hours or to desired consistency. Serve with crackers and shredded Cheddar cheese. Yield: 8 servings.

Approx Per Serving: *Cal 707; Prot 47.5 g; Carbo 44.5 g; T Fat 38.7 g; Chol 154.0 mg; Potas 1502.0 mg; Sod 2522.0 mg.*

Jim Garrison
Westminster, Colorado

ENCHILADA CASSEROLE

1 pound ground beef
1/2 cup chopped onion
1 can cream of
  mushroom soup
1 can cream of chicken
  soup
1 7-ounce can mild
  enchilada sauce
1 cup milk
1/4 cup chopped green
  chilies
6 flour tortillas
2 cups shredded
  Cheddar cheese

Brown ground beef with onion in skillet, stirring until ground beef is crumbly; drain. Add soups, enchilada sauce, milk and green chilies; mix well. Alternate layers of tortillas and beef mixture in 9x13-inch baking dish until all ingredients are used. Top with cheese. Bake at 325 degrees for 1 hour. Yield: 8 servings.

Approx Per Serving: *Cal 440; Prot 22.2 g; Carbo 28.0 g; T Fat 27.4 g; Chol 73.9 mg; Potas 297.0 mg; Sod 1241.0 mg.*

Ron M. and Sandy Ballantine
Denver, Colorado

GROUND BEEF AND POTATO CASSEROLE

Trust me: you'll like this casserole!

4 slices bacon, chopped
1 pound lean ground beef
4 pounds thin-skinned
  white potatoes
5 cloves of garlic, minced
1 teaspoon crushed bay
  leaves
2 teaspoons thyme
Pepper to taste
3 whole bay leaves
1 cup hot water

Cook bacon in skillet over medium heat until nearly crisp. Add ground beef. Cook until brown, stirring until crumbly; drain. Slice potatoes 1/4 inch thick. Place 1/5 of the slices in greased shallow 4-quart baking dish. Top with 1/4 of the beef mixture. Sprinkle with a small amount of garlic, crushed bay leaves, thyme and pepper. Repeat layers until all ingredients are used, ending with potatoes and reserving 1/2 teaspoon thyme for top. Sprinkle with reserved thyme; place whole bay leaves on top. Pour hot water over layers. Bake, covered, at 375 degrees for 1 1/2 hours or until potatoes are tender. Let stand for 15 minutes. Remove whole bay leaves. Yield: 6 servings.

Approx Per Serving: *Cal 512; Prot 22.5 g; Carbo 77.5 g; T Fat 13.1 g; Chol 52.9 mg; Potas 1469.0 mg; Sod 135.0 mg.*

Edwin A. and Shirley Bogucki
Racine, Wisconsin

QUICK AND EASY IMPROMPTU SUPPER

I always keep these ingredients on hand for unexpected company.

1 pound ground beef
1 envelope taco
  seasoning mix
1 12-ounce can Ro-Tel
  tomatoes, partially
  drained
1 pound Velveeta cheese,
  chopped
10 cups torn lettuce
2 tomatoes, chopped
1 avocado, chopped
1 purple onion, sliced
  into rings
1 8-ounce package corn
  chips

Brown ground beef in skillet, stirring until crumbly; drain. Add taco seasoning mix according to package directions. Combine tomatoes with cheese in glass dish. Microwave on High for 6 minutes, stirring after 3 minutes; mix well. Combine lettuce, tomatoes, avocado and onion in bowl; toss lightly to mix. Spoon salad onto serving plates. Layer corn chips, meat sauce and cheese sauce over salad. Serve immediately. Yield: 6 servings.

Nutritional information is not available.

Jane Ann McClain
Crockett, Texas

70

TEXAS HASH

2 large onions
1 green bell pepper
1 pound lean ground beef
1 11-ounce can tomatoes
1 12-ounce can Ro-Tel
  tomatoes
1 teaspoon chili powder
2 teaspoons salt
1/4 teaspoon pepper
3/4 cup elbow macaroni

Chop onions and green pepper. Brown ground beef with onions and green pepper in saucepan, stirring until ground beef is crumbly; drain. Add tomatoes, Ro-Tel tomatoes, chili powder, salt and pepper; mix well. Bring to a boil. Stir in uncooked macaroni; reduce heat. Simmer for 45 minutes. Yield: 8 servings.

Approx Per Serving: *Cal 889; Prot 13.2 g; Carbo 15.3 g; T Fat 8.4 g; Chol 37.0 mg; Potas 401.0 mg; Sod 702.0 mg.*

Harry Montague
Miami, Florida

DESPERADO SPAGHETTI SAUCE

This recipe was developed when I lived on a self-sufficient farm and has been refined over the years to bring ambrosia to your palate.

12 ounces lean ground beef
12 ounces Italian sausage
1 tablespoon olive oil
1 onion, chopped
4 cloves of garlic, minced
3 bay leaves
1 tablespoon oregano
1 tablespoon sweet basil
2 teaspoons aniseed
2 tablespoons sugar
2 tablespoons Sherry
1 teaspoon barbecue
  seasoning
2 teaspoons
  Worcestershire sauce
1 tablespoon parsley flakes
1 28-ounce can whole
  tomatoes
1 28-ounce can tomato
  sauce
1 6-ounce can tomato
  paste

Sauté ground beef and sausage in olive oil in stockpot over high heat until meats begin to brown. Add onion and garlic. Sauté for 3 to 4 minutes or until onion is transparent. Reduce heat. Add bay leaves, oregano, basil, aniseed, sugar, Sherry, barbecue seasoning, Worcestershire sauce, parsley flakes, tomatoes, tomato sauce, tomato paste and salt and pepper to taste; mix well. Simmer for 1 hour to 1 1/2 hours, adding water if necessary for desired consistency. Remove bay leaf. Serve over vermicelli or whole wheat spaghetti cooked *al dente*. Flavor improves if sauce is made a day ahead and reheated. Yield: 6 servings.

Approx Per Serving: *Cal 393; Prot 23.3 g; Carbo 29.2 g; T Fat 21.5 g; Chol 68.0 mg; Potas 1404.0 mg; Sod 1453.0 mg.*

Don Severa
Templeton, California

71

ITALIAN SPAGHETTI SAUCE AND CHEESE MEATBALLS

This has been a favorite dish in our family for 35 years.

1 cup chopped onion
1/2 cup chopped green
  bell pepper
2 cloves of garlic, minced
1/4 cup olive oil
2 12-ounce cans tomato
  paste
6 cups water
4 teaspoons chili powder
1 teaspoon oregano
4 teaspoons salt
1/2 teaspoon pepper
Cheese Meatballs

Sauté onion, green pepper and garlic in olive oil in heavy saucepan until transparent. Add tomato paste, water, chili powder, oregano, salt and pepper; mix well. Simmer, covered, for 30 minutes. Add Cheese Meatballs. Simmer, covered, for 30 minutes longer. Serve on hot cooked spaghetti. Yield: 10 servings.

Approx Per Serving: *Cal 116; Prot 3.0 g; Carbo 15.1 g; T Fat 6.3 g; Chol 0.0 mg; Potas 694.0 mg; Sod 908.0 mg.*
Nutritional information does not include spaghetti.

Cheese Meatballs

1 pound lean ground beef
8 ounces ground pork
  sausage
1 cup Parmesan cheese
1 cup milk
1 egg, beaten
1 cup crumbled bread
1/2 cup chopped parsley
1 large clove of garlic,
  minced
1 teaspoon salt
1/4 teaspoon pepper
1/4 cup butter

Combine ground beef, sausage, cheese, milk, egg, bread, parsley, garlic, salt and pepper in bowl; mix well. Shape into 24 meatballs. Brown in butter in skillet over low heat; drain. Yield: 10 servings.

Approx Per Serving: *Cal 328; Prot 17.3 g; Carbo 9.4 g; T Fat 24.5 g; Chol 95.0 mg; Potas 231.0 mg; Sod 672.0 mg.*

Josephine Marsh
Grand Blanc, Michigan

ITALIAN SPAGHETTI

The ground beef in this recipe "must be really brown and will resemble buckshot when done. The onions, mushrooms and peppers will have cooked away when the meat has been sufficiently browned."

2 large onions, chopped
8 ounces fresh
  mushrooms, sliced
2 green bell peppers,
  chopped
1/2 cup olive oil
2 pounds ground round
  steak
1   28-ounce can solid-
  pack tomatoes
1/4 cup chopped parsley
1 clove of garlic
1   16-ounce can tomato
  juice
1 cup red wine
1   16-ounce package
  thin spaghetti
1 cup Parmesan cheese

Sauté onions, mushrooms and green peppers in olive oil in saucepan until light brown. Add ground beef. Cook until very brown and crumbly; drain. Add tomatoes, parsley and thyme, rosemary, oregano, salt and pepper to taste. Add garlic speared on toothpick for easy removal. Simmer, covered, for 1 hour. Add tomato juice and wine. Simmer for 1 to 4 hours or to desired consistency. Remove and discard garlic. Cook spaghetti according to package directions. Drain and rinse with boiling water. Serve with sauce and cheese. Flavor improves with longer simmering. Yield: 6 servings.

Approx Per Serving: *Cal 890; Prot 45.4 g; Carbo 74.7 g; T Fat 42.8 g; Chol 97.6 mg; Potas 1368.0 mg; Sod 811.0 mg.*

Douglas B. Marshall, Gleannloch Farms
Barksdale, Texas

CURRIED HAM CASSEROLE

1   8-ounce package long
  grain and wild rice mix
1   10-ounce package
  frozen chopped broccoli
12 ounces cooked ham
1 cup cubed Cheddar
  cheese
1 can cream of celery
  soup
1 cup mayonnaise
2/3 cup evaporated milk
2 teaspoons dry mustard
3/4 teaspoon curry powder

Cook rice according to package directions. Cook broccoli according to package directions just until tender-crisp; drain well. Chop ham. Layer rice, ham, broccoli and cheese in 9x13-inch baking dish. Combine soup, mayonnaise, evaporated milk, dry mustard and curry powder in bowl; mix well. Pour over layers. Bake at 350 degrees for 45 minutes. Yield: 8 servings.

Approx Per Serving: *Cal 463; Prot 16.9 g; Carbo 27.8 g; T Fat 31.8 g; Chol 53.6 mg; Potas 313.0 mg; Sod 722.0 mg.*

Ruth Mawby
Augusta, Michigan

COUNTRY HAM

These are two old southern recipes for cooking country ham.

1 country ham
Brown sugar
Mustard
Cloves

Combine ham with water to cover in large stockpot or lard stand. Let stand overnight; drain. Cover ham with fresh water. Bring to a boil; reduce heat. Simmer for 20 minutes per pound. Remove ham to work surface. Let stand until cool enough to handle. Remove outer skin and bone. Wrap ham tightly in cloth. Store in refrigerator for several weeks. Ham will slice easily. For an alternative method, prepare ham as above and bring to a boil. Remove entire stockpot from heat and place in cardboard box well lined with newspaper. Pack with additional newspaper. Let stand for 12 to 14 hours or until cool. Trim fat from ham. Spread with a mixture of brown sugar and mustard; dot with cloves. Place in roasting pan. Bake at 350 degrees for 30 minutes.

Nutritional information is not available.

Margaret D. Fleming, Traveler's Rest Arabians
Columbia, Tennessee

HONEY AND APPLE PORK CHOPS

1$1/2$ cups apple cider
$1/4$ cup lemon juice
$1/4$ cup soy sauce
2 tablespoons honey
1 clove of garlic, minced
$1/4$ teaspoon pepper
4   8-ounce 1-inch thick
   pork chops

Combine apple cider, lemon juice, soy sauce, honey, garlic and pepper in shallow dish; mix well. Add pork chops. Marinate, covered, in refrigerator overnight, turning chops occasionally. Drain, reserving marinade. Grill pork chops 6 inches from low to medium coals for 40 to 50 minutes, turning and basting with marinade every 10 to 15 minutes. Yield: 4 servings.

Approx Per Serving: *Cal 253; Prot 16.0 g; Carbo 11.2 g; T Fat 15.9 g; Chol 58.3 mg; Potas 280.0 mg; Sod 554.0 mg.*

Holly Andersen, Rorbeck Arabians
Willis, Texas

BIGOS

This is a traditional Polish hunting dish. In the old days, it was made with venison which was marinated and put down in barrels with sauerkraut for the winter.

2 pounds sauerkraut
1 pound cabbage, shredded
5 prunes, chopped
1½ teaspoons instant
  beef bouillon
½ teaspoon caraway seed
4 slices bacon, cut into
  1-inch pieces
1 pound boneless pork,
  cut into ½-inch cubes
½ cup chopped onion
8 ounces Polish sausage
2½ cups water
1 bay leaf
¾ teaspoon paprika
1 6-ounce can tomato
  paste
¼ cup dry red wine

Rinse sauerkraut; drain. Combine sauerkraut with a small amount of boiling water in 3-quart saucepan. Cook for 5 minutes. Stir in shredded cabbage, prunes, bouillon, caraway seed and salt to taste. Simmer, covered, for 2 hours or until tender. Brown bacon in saucepan; remove to drain. Brown pork and onion in bacon drippings in saucepan. Slice sausage. Stir bacon, sausage, 2½ cups water, bay leaf and paprika into saucepan. Simmer, covered, for 1 hour or until pork is tender. Remove bay leaf. Add to sauerkraut mixture; mix well. Stir in tomato paste and wine. Cook for 10 minutes. Yield: 8 servings.

Approx Per Serving: *Cal 272; Prot 16.4 g; Carbo 16.0 g; T Fat 16.1 g; Chol 55.6 mg; Potas 727.0 mg; Sod 1272.0 mg.*

Andre Pater
Lexington, Kentucky

ARABIAN KUFTA

This is an Arabian recipe for grilled lamb meatballs in a yogurt sauce.

2 pounds lean lamb
2 large onions
¾ cup chopped Italian
  parsley
2 tablespoons milk
1 teaspoon thyme
1 teaspoon cumin
1 teaspoon salt
1 teaspoon pepper
3 tomatoes
2 day-old pita bread
  rounds, toasted
2 tablespoons meat broth
16 ounces yogurt

Put lamb, onions and parsley through meat grinder. Combine with milk and seasonings in bowl; mix well by hand. Shape into 1-inch meatballs; flatten slightly. Grill over hot coals until cooked through. Peel, seed and chop tomatoes. Cook to desired consistency in butter in skillet. Crumble pita bread into warmed serving dish. Spoon tomatoes and broth over bread. Beat yogurt in bowl until smooth. Spoon over bread. Arrange meatballs in yogurt. Garnish with sliced tomato, chopped green pepper and additional chopped parsley. Yield: 6 servings.

Nutritional information is not available.

*Excerpted from **Aramco World***

BENGAL CURRY WITH PLUM CHUTNEY

2 pounds boneless lamb
  shoulder
2 tablespoons shortening
1/2 cup sliced onion
1 tablespoon curry
  powder
1/8 teaspoon cloves
1 teaspoon salt
1/8 teaspoon pepper
2 tablespoons slivered
  crystallized ginger
1 tablespoon chopped
  mint
2 cups milk
2 tablespoons flour
1/2 cup cold water
1/2 cup coconut
2 tablespoons lime juice
1 cup light cream
3 cups cooked rice

Cut lamb into 1-inch cubes. Brown in shortening in large heavy saucepan. Add onion. Sauté for 5 minutes. Stir in mixture of curry powder, cloves, salt and pepper. Add ginger, mint and milk. Bring to a boil; reduce heat. Simmer, covered, for 1 hour or until lamb is tender. Mixture will appear curdled. Blend flour and water in cup. Stir gradually into lamb mixture. Bring to a boil, stirring constantly; remove from heat. Stir in coconut, lime juice and cream. Heat just to serving temperature. Serve over rice with toppings such as Plum Chutney, chopped hard-boiled eggs, coconut, pineapple, avocado, tomatoes, crisp bacon, green onions or peanuts. Yield: 4 servings.

Approx Per Serving: *Cal 1012; Prot 51.5 g; Carbo 56.5 g; T Fat 63.8 g; Chol 244.0 mg; Potas 792.0 mg; Sod 728.0 mg.*

Plum Chutney

5 pounds purple plums
2 pounds yellow onions,
  chopped
4 pounds McIntosh
  apples, peeled, chopped
3 cups white vinegar
2 pounds sugar
2 pounds dark brown
  sugar
1 tablespoon allspice
1 tablespoon cloves
1 tablespoon ginger
1 teaspoon cayenne
  pepper
3 tablespoons salt

Peel plums and cut into halves. Combine with onions, apples and vinegar in large saucepan. Bring to a boil. Stir in sugar, brown sugar, allspice, cloves, ginger, cayenne pepper and salt. Simmer for 1 1/2 hours, stirring occasionally. Ladle into hot sterilized 1-pint jars, leaving 1/2-inch headspace; seal with 2-piece lids. Serve with curry dishes, chicken, duck or barbecued pork. Yield: 20 cups.

Approx Per Cup: *Cal 478; Prot 1.5 g; Carbo 123.0 g; T Fat 1.2 g; Chol 0.0 mg; Potas 552.0 mg; Sod 987.0 mg.*

Patricia J. Miller
Winnemucca, Nevada

LAMB SHANKS DRENNAN

Serve sauce over mashed potatoes. Be sure to have lots of mint jelly.

4 lamb shanks
1/2 cup butter
2 medium onions, sliced
1/2 cup dry white wine
1/2 cup tomato juice
1 cup chicken broth
1 teaspoon paprika
1 teaspoon ginger
1 teaspoon salt
1/2 teaspoon pepper

Trim lamb shanks. Brown well in butter in large skillet. Remove to baking dish. Sauté onions in pan drippings in skillet. Stir in wine, tomato juice, broth, paprika, ginger, salt and pepper. Cook for several minutes, stirring to mix well. Pour over lamb. Bake, covered, at 250 degrees for 3 hours or until very tender. Yield: 4 servings.

Approx Per Serving: *Cal 506; Prot 28.3 g; Carbo 8.4 g; T Fat 38.8 g; Chol 153.0 mg; Potas 608.0 mg; Sod 1100.0 mg.*

Mrs. Lee Bossen
Clinton, Iowa

ESTOFADO

This is a Spanish stew. Serve with spinach salad, toasted garlic bread and Parmesan cheese.

1 pound lean boneless
  lamb
1 large onion, sliced
1 green bell pepper
1 tablespoon olive oil
1 cup dry red wine
1 cup chopped tomatoes
1/4 cup golden raisins
1/4 cup chopped dried
  apricots
1 clove of garlic, minced
1 1/2 teaspoons salt
1/8 teaspoon pepper
1 teaspoon basil
1 teaspoon thyme
1 teaspoon tarragon
1 bay leaf
1/2 cup sliced mushrooms
1/4 cup sliced black olives
1 tablespoon flour
1 cup cold water

Cut lamb into 1-inch cubes. Slice onion 1/4-inch thick; cut green pepper into strips. Brown lamb in olive oil in large saucepan. Add wine, tomatoes, onion, green pepper, raisins, apricots, garlic, salt, pepper and spices; mix well. Simmer, covered, for 1 hour. Add mushrooms and olives. Simmer for 30 minutes longer. Blend flour and water in small bowl. Stir into stew. Cook until thickened, stirring constantly. Remove bay leaf. Serve over white or brown rice or couscous. Yield: 6 servings.

Approx Per Serving: *Cal 270; Prot 13.9 g; Carbo 16.0 g; T Fat 15.6 g; Chol 42.8 mg; Potas 503.0 mg; Sod 718.0 mg.*

Carol McEwen, Jameel Farm
Augusta, Kansas

Talley Ho!

BARBECUED BEAR

1   4-pound bear roast
1/2 teaspoon salt
1/2 teaspoon garlic salt
1/2 teaspoon pepper
1 cup tomato juice
1/2 cup water
1/4 cup catsup
1/4 cup vinegar
2 tablespoons
   Worcestershire sauce
2 tablespoons brown sugar
1 tablespoon paprika
1 teaspoon dry mustard
1/4 teaspoon chili powder
1/8 teaspoon red pepper

Season roast with salt, garlic salt and pepper. Place in roasting pan. Roast at 350 degrees until meat thermometer registers well done. Combine tomato juice, water, catsup, vinegar, Worcestershire sauce, brown sugar, paprika, dry mustard, chili powder and cayenne pepper in bowl; mix well. Slice roast. Place in shallow baking dish. Pour sauce over top. Marinate in refrigerator overnight. Reheat in sauce to serve. Everyone who eats this thinks that it is roast beef. Yield: 8 servings.

Nutritional information is not available.

Grant and Joyce Johnson
Fargo, North Dakota

FAVORITE VENISON RECIPE

This tasty recipe tastes like teriyaki.

1 pound venison
2 tablespoons oil
1/4 cup soy sauce
2 teaspoons sugar
1 tablespoon oil

Cut venison into bite-sized pieces. Combine with 2 tablespoons oil, soy sauce and sugar in bowl. Marinate for 1 hour or longer; drain. Brown quickly in 1 tablespoon oil in skillet. Serve on rice or noodles. Yield: 4 servings.

Approx Per Serving: *Cal 190; Prot 17.7 g; Carbo 3.6 g; T Fat 11.5 g; Chol 36.9 mg; Potas 223.0 mg; Sod 1069.0 mg.*

Theresa Ferland Blaisdell, Thistledown Farm
Lunenburg, Vermont

RABBIT SAUCE PIQUANT

1   16-ounce bottle of Newman's Own salad dressing
3 tablespoons Creole seasoning
4 cloves of garlic, minced
1 tablespoon Worcestershire sauce
1 tablespoon hot sauce
1/2 teaspoon white pepper
18 pieces rabbit, boned
3/4 cup olive oil
6 onions
3 bunches green onions
1 green bell pepper
4 stalks celery, chopped
1   12-ounce can Ro-Tel tomatoes
2   6-ounce cans tomato paste
1 can cream of mushroom soup
4 soup cans water
1 cup dry red wine

Combine salad dressing, Creole seasoning, garlic, Worcestershire sauce, hot sauce and white pepper in bowl. Add rabbit; mix well. Marinate in refrigerator for 12 hours; drain. Brown rabbit in olive oil in saucepan. Remove rabbit to paper towel to drain. Chop onions, green onions and green pepper finely. Sauté onions, green onions, green pepper and celery in pan drippings in saucepan. Add mixture of tomatoes, tomato paste and soup; mix well. Stir in water and wine. Simmer for 45 minutes. Add rabbit. Cook until rabbit is very tender. Yield: 10 servings.

Approx Per Serving: *Cal 638; Prot 26.0 g; Carbo 25.7 g; T Fat 51.9 g; Chol 69.8 mg; Potas 974.0 mg; Sod 608.0 mg.*

Phil Witter, Live Oak Arabians
Baton Rouge, Louisiana

DUCK STROGANOFF

2 mallard ducks, cut up
1 tablespoon flour
1 1/2 teaspoons salt
1/2 teaspoon pepper
3 tablespoons olive oil
3 tablespoons butter
1 large white onion
1/2 teaspoon thyme
1/2 teaspoon sweet basil
1/2 teaspoon parsley
   flakes
1 cup Sauterne
1 cup whipping cream

Coat ducks with mixture of flour, salt and pepper. Brown in olive oil and butter in Dutch oven. Chop onion. Add onion, thyme, basil and parsley. Heat wine in small saucepan. Add to ducks. Bake, covered, at 350 degrees for 1 hour. Stir in cream. Bake for 20 to 25 minutes longer. Mixture will appear curdled. Serve over rice. Yield: 6 servings.

Approx Per Serving: *Cal 517; Prot 28.0 g; Carbo 4.6 g; T Fat 40.0 g; Chol 171.0 mg; Potas 393.0 mg; Sod 672.0 mg.*

Grant and Joyce Johnson
Fargo, North Dakota

WILD GOOSE

This is an old Danish family recipe. The goose will always be tender and the sauce is delicious. It can also be prepared with 2 wild ducks.

1 wild goose
1/4 cup butter
2 tablespoons sugar
1/2 cup butter
1/2 cup flour
2 tablespoons currant
   jelly
2 cups heavy cream

Cut goose into pieces, discarding skin. Rinse well and pat dry. Brown on both sides in 1/4 cup butter and sugar in Dutch oven. Season with salt and pepper to taste. Add water to nearly cover. Simmer, covered, for 1 hour and 15 minutes. Drain and reserve cooking liquid. Melt 1/2 cup butter in saucepan. Blend in flour. Stir in reserved cooking liquid and jelly. Cook until thickened and smooth, stirring constantly. Stir in cream. Pour over goose in Dutch oven. Bake at 300 degrees for 1 to 1 1/2 hours or until goose is tender. Yield: 6 servings.

Approx Per Serving: *Cal 727; Prot 24.8 g; Carbo 18.5 g; T Fat 62.0 g; Chol 244.0 mg; Potas 375.0 mg; Sod 282.0 mg.*

Rita Clausen
Spokane, Washington

This is absolutely the best wild turkey recipe. It is very tender and tasty.

1 wild turkey
Vinegar
Water
1 orange
1 apple
Salt and pepper
Stuffing
Butter
Milk

Wash turkey inside and out; pat dry. Combine with equal amounts of vinegar and water in large bowl. Soak for 1 hour, turning once. Drain and rinse well. Place orange and apple in cavity. Season cavity with salt and pepper to taste. Stuff as desired. Place in roasting pan. Brush with butter. Bake at 350 degrees for 1 hour, basting with butter every 15 minutes. Pour 1 1/2 inches milk in roasting pan. Bake, covered, for 2 hours longer.

Nutritional information is not available.

Peggy Yates
Mayhill, New Mexico

AKOORI

This is a spicy omelet which originated with the Parsis in India.

1 large onion, thinly sliced
2 tablespoons oil
1/4 teaspoon turmeric
1/2 teaspoon cumin
1/4 teaspoon coriander
1/2 teaspoon chopped
   peeled ginger
1 green chili, chopped
1 large tomato, chopped
1 tablespoon finely
   chopped fresh parsley
6 eggs

Sauté onion in oil in nonstick skillet. Add turmeric, cumin and coriander. Cook until light brown. Add ginger, green chili, tomato and parsley. Sauté just until tomato is soft. Beat eggs with salt and pepper to taste in bowl. Pour into skillet. Cook over low heat until eggs begin to set and form soft mounds, stirring gently. Remove from heat. Let stand until set. Serve immediately with Indian bread or French bread. Yield: 4 servings.

Approx Per Serving: *Cal 205; Prot 10.2 g; Carbo 6.6 g; T Fat 15.5 g; Chol 411.0 mg; Potas 274.0 mg; Sod 108.0 mg.*

Elizabeth Gazder
London, England

ARABIAN RED LENTILS AND RICE

Add chopped meat, fish, hard-boiled eggs or cheese to add variety to this staple.

1 cup dried red lentils
4 cups water or broth
2 teaspoons salt
2 yellow onions
1/4 cup olive oil
1/2 cup uncooked rice
1/4 teaspoon pepper
1 teaspoon curry powder

Wash and sort lentils. Combine lentils, water and salt in large heavy saucepan. Bring to a boil; reduce heat. Simmer for 20 minutes. Slice onions thinly. Sauté in olive oil in heavy skillet until golden. Add to lentils. Add rice, pepper and curry powder. Simmer, covered, for 20 minutes or until rice is tender, stirring frequently and adding water or broth as necessary. Mixture should be consistency of applesauce. Garnish with chopped fresh parsley. Yield: 6 servings.

Nutritional information is not available.

*Excerpted from **Aramco World***

82

GREEN CHILI ENCHILADAS

I grow my own green chilies or bring them back from Mexico.

2 cans cream of chicken
  soup
1/2 soup can water
1/2 soup can milk
2 tablespoons flour
1 cup chopped green
  chilies
1 clove of garlic, crushed
12 corn tortillas
1 1/2 cups shredded
  Monterey Jack cheese
1 1/2 cups shredded sharp
  Cheddar cheese
1 medium onion, chopped
2 cups sour cream
4 poached eggs

Blend first 4 ingredients in saucepan. Cook until slightly thickened, stirring constantly. Add green chilies, garlic and salt to taste. Heat until bubbly. Wrap tortillas in foil. Heat in oven just until warm. Combine 1 cup Monterey Jack cheese and 1 cup Cheddar cheese with onion and sour cream in bowl; mix well. Place 1 spoonful soup mixture and 1 spoonful cheese sauce on each of 4 warmed serving plates. Top with 1 tortilla. Repeat layers until all ingredients are used. Bake at 375 degrees just until cheese is melted. Top each serving with 1 egg. Sprinkle with remaining cheeses. Bake just until cheese is melted. Serve with lettuce and tomato. Yield: 4 servings.

Approx Per Serving: *Cal 1059; Prot 43.8 g; Carbo 68.1 g; T Fat 70.1 g; Chol 426.0 mg; Potas 790.0 mg; Sod 1842.0 mg.*

Jennifer Jo Bird, Jen-Mar Arabians
Manor, Texas

KHEMOSABI QUICHE

This is a quiche that real men will eat.

1/2 cup butter
2 large brown onions
8 ounces mushrooms
1/2 ounce dry vermouth
2 tablespoons minced
  garlic
1 cup shredded Cheddar
  cheese
1 cup shredded
  Monterey Jack cheese
2 unbaked pie shells
6 eggs
1 cup whipping cream
1 tablespoon
  Worcestershire sauce

Melt butter in skillet. Chop onions and slice mushrooms. Add wine and garlic to skillet. Add onions and mushrooms. Sauté until golden. Reserve 2 tablespoons of each cheese. Alternate layers of remaining cheeses and mushroom mixture in 9-inch pie shells until all ingredients are used. Combine eggs, cream and Worcestershire sauce in bowl; mix with wire whisk. Pour over layers in pie shells. Top with reserved cheeses. Bake at 350 degrees for 45 minutes. Serve warm or cold. May reheat in microwave if desired. Yield: 12 servings.

Approx Per Serving: *Cal 455; Prot 13.3 g; Carbo 18.4 g; T Fat 36.8 g; Chol 212.0 mg; Potas 227.0 mg; Sod 463.0 mg.*

B. Paul Husband
Saugus, California

CORN AND SAUSAGE CHOWDER

I serve this chowder with a green salad and toasted pita bread.

2 pounds medium or hot
  sausage
10 new potatoes, cut into
  quarters
1 cup chopped onion
1/2 cup chopped green
  bell pepper
2 16-ounce cans
  tomatoes
2 16-ounce cans cream-
  style corn
1 tablespoon minced
  parsley
1 teaspoon basil
1 1/2 teaspoons salt
1/2 teaspoon pepper
2 cups half and half
2 tablespoons flour

Brown sausage in heavy saucepan over medium heat. Drain all but 1 tablespoon drippings. Add potatoes, onion, green pepper and tomatoes. Simmer, covered, for 15 minutes or until vegetables are tender, adding 1/2 cup water if necessary for desired consistency. Stir in corn, parsley, basil, salt and pepper. Shake half and half and flour in jar to blend. Stir into chowder. Cook until thickened, stirring constantly. Serve immediately or store in refrigerator and reheat. Flavor improves on second day. Yield: 8 servings.

Approx Per Serving: *Cal 731; Prot 20.4 g; Carbo 45.4 g; T Fat 53.7 g; Chol 99.8 mg; Potas 1019.0 mg; Sod 1706.0 mg.*

Carol McEwen, Jameel Farm
Augusta, Kansas

MINESTRONE FROM DETROIT

This recipe is from an old family-style Italian restaurant in downtown Detroit.

2 12-ounce cans beef
  bouillon
4 to 6 bouillon cans water
8 carrots, sliced
1 bunch celery with
  leaves, chopped
3 onions, finely chopped
1 16-ounce can kidney
  beans
1 28-ounce can stewed
  tomatoes
6 potatoes, peeled,
  chopped
7 cups milk

Combine bouillon, 4 to 6 cans water, carrots, celery, onions, undrained kidney beans and tomatoes. Bring to a boil over medium heat. Place potatoes in blender container with small amount of water. Process until smooth, adding additional water as needed. Stir into soup. Simmer over medium heat for 5 hours, stirring every 15 minutes. Add salt and pepper to taste. May add water if needed for desired consistency. Ladle into soup bowls. Add 1/2 cup milk to each bowl. Yield: 14 servings.

Approx Per Serving: *Cal 213; Prot 9.2 g; Carbo 35.3 g; T Fat 4.7 g; Chol 16.6 mg; Potas 943.0 mg; Sod 463.0 mg.*

Judy W. Jones
Sioux City, Iowa

VERMONT CORN CHOWDER

This is especially good served with corn bread.

1 cup chopped onion
1/2 cup chopped celery
2 tablespoons butter
2 cups milk
2 cups cream-style corn
3 cups chopped cooked
  potatoes
2 cups shredded
  Cheddar cheese

Sauté onion and celery in butter in large stockpot until tender. Add milk, corn, potatoes, and salt and pepper to taste. Heat just to serving temperature. Remove from heat. Stir in cheese until melted, returning to very low heat if necessary. Garnish with parsley. Yield: 7 servings.

Approx Per Serving: *Cal 354; Prot 13.9 g; Carbo 39.8 g; T Fat 16.8 g; Chol 52.3 mg; Potas 664.0 mg; Sod 479.0 mg.*

Theresa Ferland Blaisdell, Thistledown Farm
Lunenburg, Vermont

TEN-BEAN SOUP

This recipe is from my twin sister who lives in southern California. You may substitute 1 pound of ham hocks for chicken.

1/4 cup dried black-eyed
  peas
1/4 cup dried Great
  Northern beans
1/4 cup dried split peas
1/4 cup dried yellow split
  peas
1/4 cup dried navy beans
1/4 cup dried pinto beans
1/4 cup dried black beans
1/4 cup dried red beans
1/4 cup dried lima beans
1/4 cup dried lentils
1 chicken
1 large potato, chopped
1 large carrot, chopped
1 cup chopped celery
1 small onion, chopped
1 16-ounce can whole
  kernel corn

Soak dried beans in water to cover overnight. Cook chicken in water to cover in large saucepan until meat falls from bones. Drain, reserving stock. Chill chicken in refrigerator. Chop chicken, discarding skin and bones. Combine chicken and reserved stock in 8-quart stockpot. Process potato and carrot in blender or food processor container until finely chopped. Add to soup with celery, onion and undrained corn. Add beans and enough water for desired consistency. Simmer for several hours or until beans are tender and soup is thickened to desired consistency. Season with salt and pepper to taste. Yield: 16 servings.

Approx Per Serving: *Cal 208; Prot 19.6 g; Carbo 24.8 g; T Fat 3.8 g; Chol 38.0 mg; Potas 527.0 mg; Sod 114.0 mg.*

Judy W. Jones
Sioux City, Iowa

On The Wing

WILD AMERICA'S EASY CHICKEN

We have made this easy recipe for years. It can also be made with brown rice, but it requires additional water and cooking time.

1 chicken
1 onion, chopped
1 cup rice
¹/₂ cup butter

Rinse chicken and pat dry. Combine with onion and water to cover in saucepan. Cook for 2 hours or until tender. Drain and bone chicken. Brown rice in butter in skillet for 5 minutes. Combine boned chicken, rice and skillet drippings in baking dish. Bake at 350 degrees for 1 hour. Yield: 6 servings.

Approx Per Serving: *Cal 472; Prot 35.3 g; Carbo 26.8 g; T Fat 23.9 g; Chol 143.0 mg; Potas 350.0 mg; Sod 228.0 mg.*

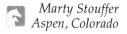 *Marty Stouffer
Aspen, Colorado*

CHICKEN BY DOM

There isn't a horse in town that wouldn't run two miles in a minute for seconds of this terrific dish, which is also very good the first time around! Look for my cookbook "Eat This" in bookstores.

8 chicken breast filets
2 tablespoons freshly
  grated ginger
2 bunches scallions,
  chopped
1/4 cup butter
1 cup chicken stock
2 7-ounce cans sliced
  water chestnuts,
  drained
1 pound fresh button
  mushrooms, cut into
  quarters
Pepper to taste
2 cups sour cream
6 cups cooked brown rice
1 cup sour cream

Rinse chicken and pat dry. Cut into bite-sized pieces. Sauté chicken, ginger and scallions in butter in large skillet. Add chicken stock. Bring just to the boiling point; reduce heat. Simmer just until chicken is cooked through. Add water chestnuts, mushrooms and pepper. Simmer for 2 minutes, stirring gently. Stir in 2 cups sour cream. Cook until heated through, stirring to mix well. Serve over rice. Top each serving with 2 tablespoons sour cream. Garnish with chopped fresh parsley. Yield: 8 servings.

Approx Per Serving: *Cal 628; Prot 34.5 g; Carbo 51.3 g; T Fat 31.8 g; Chol 126.0 mg; Potas 796.0 mg; Sod 259.0 mg.*

Dom DeLuise
Beverly Hills, California

ARABIAN CHICKEN AND RICE (Al Roaz Al Zirbeyan)

5 onions, chopped
1/4 cup oil
1 cup yogurt
3 cups tomato juice
1/2 teaspoon cinnamon
1/2 teaspoon cardamom
1/2 teaspoon pepper
2 chickens, cut up
2 hot peppers or green
  chili peppers, chopped
5 cups rice
1 teaspoon turmeric
1 tablespoon oil

Sauté onions in 1/4 cup oil in large skillet. Remove onions with slotted spoon; drain. Combine onions with yogurt, tomato juice, cinnamon, cardamom, pepper and salt to taste in saucepan. Rinse chicken and pat dry. Brown in drippings in skillet. Add chicken and peppers to yogurt mixture. Simmer until chicken is tender. Cook rice with salt to taste in water in saucepan until partially cooked; drain. Stir in turmeric. Layer half the rice, chicken mixture and remaining rice in saucepan. Drizzle with 1 tablespoon oil. Simmer for 1 hour or until tender. Serve hot. Yield: 10 servings.

Nutritional information is not available.

*Excerpted from **Aramco World***

REED HAWN'S WORLD FAMOUS BARBECUED CHICKEN

I've been making this chicken for many years and never had a complaint. This is good for those concerned about too much beef, but you can always sneak in a steak or two for us red meat lovers.

1 32-ounce bottle of catsup
1/4 cup (or more) Worcestershire sauce
1/4 cup (or more) steak sauce
1/3 cup (or more) sugar
Juice of 1 lemon
1/2 cup butter
6 chicken halves

Combine catsup, Worcestershire sauce, steak sauce, sugar, lemon juice and butter in saucepan. Simmer until well blended. Rinse chicken and pat dry. Season to taste. Place on grill over medium coals. Cook, with grill cover closed, for 20 to 30 minutes or until chicken is partially done, turning chicken frequently. Brush generously with sauce. Cook for 20 to 30 minutes longer or until chicken tests done, basting frequently with sauce. Yield: 8 servings.

Approx Per Serving: *Cal 754; Prot 76.4 g; Carbo 40.1 g; T Fat 30.9 g; Chol 259.0 mg; Potas 1102.0 mg; Sod 1571.0 mg.*

Reed Hawn, Hawn Arabians
Austin, Texas

SOUTHWESTERN BARBECUED CHICKEN

Serve with fresh salsa, hot flour tortillas, ranch-style beans and Corona beer.

1/4 cup butter
1/4 cup molasses
1 clove of garlic, crushed
1/2 teaspoon paprika
2 teaspoons tarragon vinegar
3/4 cup catsup
1 tablespoon Worcestershire sauce
1 teaspoon mustard
1 teaspoon salt
1/4 teaspoon pepper
2 3-pound chickens, cut into halves

Combine butter, molasses, garlic, paprika, vinegar, catsup, Worcestershire sauce, mustard, salt and pepper in saucepan. Simmer for 20 minutes, stirring frequently. Rinse chicken and pat dry. Break joints. Rub with salt, pepper and chili powder to taste. Place skin side up on grill 3 inches from hot coals. Cook for 30 minutes on each side, basting frequently with barbecue sauce. Yield: 6 servings.

Approx Per Serving: *Cal 567; Prot 66.4 g; Carbo 16.7 g; T Fat 24.7 g; Chol 223.0 mg; Potas 824.0 mg; Sod 1007.0 mg.*

Mike Villasenor
Valley Center, California

ALMOND CHICKEN

This easy recipe is a favorite with company and the man of the house. Serve with your favorite rice.

1½ cups water
2 tablespoons dry Sherry
1½ tablespoons cornstarch
4 teaspoons soy sauce
1 teaspoon instant
  chicken bouillon granules
2 tablespoons Sherry
1 tablespoon cornstarch
1 egg white
½ teaspoon salt
4 whole chicken breasts
3 cups oil
½ cup blanched almonds
1 teaspoon grated fresh
  ginger root
1 large carrot, finely
  chopped
6 green onions, cut into
  1-inch pieces
3 stalks celery,
  diagonally cut into
  ½-inch slices
8 mushrooms
½ cup drained sliced
  bamboo shoots

Combine water, 2 tablespoons Sherry, 1½ tablespoons cornstarch, soy sauce and bouillon granules in saucepan. Simmer for 5 minutes or until thickened, stirring constantly. Keep warm. Mix 2 tablespoons Sherry, 1 tablespoon cornstarch, egg white and salt in large bowl. Skin chicken; rinse and pat dry. Cut into 1-inch pieces. Add to egg white mixture. Heat oil to 375 degrees in wok. Cook ⅓ of the pieces at a time for 3 to 5 minutes or until light brown; drain on paper towels. Drain all but 2 tablespoons oil from wok. Stir-fry almonds for 2 minutes or until golden brown; drain. Add ginger and carrot to wok. Stir-fry for 1 minute. Add onions, celery, mushrooms and bamboo shoots. Stir-fry for 3 minutes or just until tender-crisp. Add chicken, almonds and warm sauce. Heat to serving temperature. Yield: 6 servings.

Nutritional information is not available.

Donna L. Jensen
Bradenton, Florida

CHICKEN WITH BLEU CHEESE SAUCE

6 chicken breast filets
¼ cup butter
8 ounces sour cream
4 ounces bleu cheese
1½ teaspoons
  Worcestershire sauce
1 clove of garlic, crushed

Rinse chicken and pat dry. Brown on both sides in butter in large skillet. Place in greased 9x13-inch baking dish. Combine sour cream, bleu cheese, Worcestershire sauce and garlic in small mixer bowl; mix well. Spoon over chicken. Bake for 50 minutes or until tender. Yield: 6 servings.

Approx Per Serving: *Cal 385; Prot 30.7 g; Carbo 2.5 g; T Fat 27.6 g; Chol 123.0 mg; Potas 326.0 mg; Sod 420.0 mg.*

Debby Cain
Oregon, Illinois

BLACKHAWK CHICKEN

16 chicken breast filets
16 slices ham
16 1/2x1x21/2-inch sticks
  Swiss cheese
1/2 cup flour
3 eggs, beaten
3 cups bread crumbs
1/2 cup butter
6 tablespoons Cognac
1 cup whipping cream

Rinse chicken and pat dry. Flatten between waxed paper with meat mallet. Place 1 slice ham and 1 piece cheese on each chicken breast. Wrap chicken to enclose ham and cheese. Coat with flour seasoned with salt and pepper to taste. Dip in eggs; roll in bread crumbs. Chill for 1 hour or longer. Brown chicken on both sides in butter in skillet. Arrange in baking dish. Bake at 350 degrees for 10 minutes or just until chicken is tender. Remove to serving dish. Add Cognac to pan drippings. Ignite; allow flame to die. Stir in cream and salt and pepper to taste. Simmer until thickened, stirring constantly. Pour over chicken. Yield: 16 servings.

Approx Per Serving: *Cal 431; Prot 35.9 g; Carbo 15.3 g; T Fat 24.5 g; Chol 166.0 mg; Potas 360.0 mg; Sod 652.0 mg.*

Lynne Sebelius Halpenny
Bieber, California

CHICKEN CASTO BRATO

3 whole chicken breasts
2 cloves of garlic, minced
1 onion, cut into quarters
1 tablespoon oil
1 20-ounce can sliced
  pineapple
11/2 teaspoons cumin
11/2 teaspoons cinnamon
1 8-ounce can tomatoes
1 cup black olives
1 cup green olives
1/2 cup salsa
2 tablespoons cornstarch
1 green bell pepper,
  chopped

Rinse chicken and pat dry. Sauté garlic and onion in oil in skillet. Add chicken. Cook until brown on sides. Drain pineapple, reserving juice. Add reserved juice, cumin and cinnamon to chicken. Add tomatoes, black olives, green olives and salsa. Simmer for 20 minutes or until chicken is tender. Stir in cornstarch if needed for desired consistency. Cook until thickened, stirring constantly. Stir in green pepper and pineapple. Serve over rice. Yield: 6 servings.

Approx Per Serving: *Cal 407; Prot 27.6 g; Carbo 28.5 g; T Fat 23.9 g; Chol 72.0 mg; Potas 530.0 mg; Sod 1336.0 mg.*

Ruth Boyd
Denver, Colorado

CHINESE CHICKEN

Olive oil for frying
2 pounds chicken breast
  filets, chopped
2 cloves of garlic, minced
1 onion, finely chopped
1 teaspoon garlic salt
1 tablespoon onion salt
1/4 cup soy sauce
1/8 teaspoon each salt,
  pepper
1 green bell pepper
3 stalks celery, sliced
1/2 cup margarine
1   8-ounce can Chinese
  vegetables
1   8-ounce can mushrooms
1/2 package dry onion
  soup mix
1/2 cup water

Pour 1/4-inch olive oil into skillet. Brown chicken, garlic and onion in hot oil, stirring frequently. Season with garlic salt, onion salt, soy sauce, salt and pepper. Cut green pepper into strips. Add green pepper, celery, margarine and Chinese vegetables to skillet. Simmer for 15 minutes, stirring frequently. Add drained mushrooms and mixture of onion soup mix and 1/2 cup water. Simmer for 10 to 15 minutes or until chicken is tender, stirring occasionally. Serve over cooked rice. Yield: 6 servings.

Nutritional information is not available.

Robert Giannunzio
Vulcan, Michigan

CHICKEN DELICIOUS

This was my mother's recipe. I like the rice cooked in chicken broth when possible.

1 cup chopped celery
3/4 cup mayonnaise
1 tablespoon onion flakes
1 tablespoon lemon juice
1 can cream of chicken
  soup
1 teaspoon salt
1 cup cooked rice
1   7-ounce can sliced
  water chestnuts
3 cups chopped cooked
  chicken
1 1/2 cups cornflakes
3/4 cup slivered almonds
1/2 cup melted butter

Cook celery in water to cover in saucepan for 10 minutes; drain. Combine mayonnaise, onion flakes, lemon juice, soup and salt in bowl; mix well. Add rice, celery, drained water chestnuts and chicken; mix well. Spoon into 9x13-inch baking dish sprayed with nonstick cooking spray. Chill until ready to bake if desired. Sprinkle with cornflakes and almonds. Drizzle with melted butter. Bake at 350 degrees for 35 minutes. Yield: 8 servings.

Approx Per Serving: *Cal 525; Prot 20.3 g; Carbo 19.6 g; T Fat 41.4 g; Chol 81.0 mg; Potas 351.0 mg; Sod 978.0 mg.*

Bliss Brown, Paramont Arabians
Abingdon, Virginia

CHICKEN CORDON BLEU

Breaded chicken rolls may be stored in refrigerator or freezer until you are ready to cook them.

1 pound chicken breast filets
4 ounces thinly sliced ham
4 ounces thinly sliced Swiss cheese
1 egg, beaten
1/2 cup Italian bread crumbs
3 tablespoons butter
1   12-ounce jar home-style chicken gravy
1 cup white wine
1½ cups sliced mushrooms
1 tablespoon parsley flakes

Rinse chicken and pat dry. Flatten to 3/8-inch thickness. Layer ham and cheese on chicken. Roll up chicken to enclose ham and cheese; secure with toothpicks. Dip in beaten egg; coat with bread crumbs. Brown in butter in skillet over low heat. Place in deep baking dish. Top with chicken gravy, wine and mushrooms. Sprinkle with parsley flakes. Bake, covered with foil, at 350 degrees for 45 minutes or until tender. Yield: 4 servings.

Approx Per Serving: *Cal 602; Prot 45.0 g; Carbo 16.5 g; T Fat 34.8 g; Chol 210.0 mg; Potas 591.0 mg; Sod 1147.0 mg.*

Joanne Martin
Ontario, New York

CHICKEN ENCHILADA WITH SPANISH SAUCE

1 small onion, chopped
1 tablespoon oil
2   8-ounce cans tomato sauce
1/4 cup water
1 tablespoon chili powder
1 teaspoon salt
12 corn tortillas
3 cups chopped cooked chicken
3 cups shredded Cheddar cheese

Sauté onion in oil in saucepan. Add tomato sauce, water, chili powder and salt. Simmer for 20 minutes. Dip tortillas 1 at a time in sauce. Place chicken on tortillas. Roll to enclose chicken. Place in baking dish. Top with cheese and remaining sauce. Bake at 350 degrees just until cheese is melted. Serve immediately. Yield: 12 servings.

Approx Per Serving: *Cal 242; Prot 18.8 g; Carbo 11.3 g; T Fat 13.8 g; Chol 61.0 mg; Potas 293.0 mg; Sod 612.0 mg.*

Rosalinda Reyes, Donoghue Arabian Farm
Goliad, Texas

WHITE CHICKEN CHILI

4 chicken breasts
7 corn tortillas
2 tablespoons oil
1 7-ounce bottle of taco
  sauce
1 4-ounce can chopped
  green chilies
1 12-ounce can small
  white corn
1 pound Monterey Jack
  cheese, shredded
1 12-ounce can sliced
  green olives
1 bunch green onions
1 cup Parmesan cheese
8 ounces whipping cream

Cook and shred chicken. Cut tortillas into 3/8-inch strips. Sauté tortilla strips several at a time in hot oil in skillet just until limp; drain on paper towels. Place 1/3 of the tortillas in 7x11-inch baking dish. Combine taco sauce, green chilies and corn in bowl; mix well. Layer chicken, Monterey Jack cheese, taco sauce mixture, olives, chopped green onions and remaining tortilla strips 1/2 at a time in baking dish. Sprinkle with Parmesan cheese. Bake at 350 degrees for 15 minutes. Pour cream over top. Bake for 45 minutes longer. May substitute Mexicorn for white corn and 1/2 cup sour cream for half the whipping cream. Yield: 6 servings.

Approx Per Serving: *Cal 837; Prot 47.0 g; Carbo 34.1 g; T Fat 60.3 g; Chol 180.0 mg; Potas 578.0 mg; Sod 2417.0 mg.*

Debby Wood
Beverly Hills, California

EMPRESS ARABIANS COMPANY CHICKEN

8 chicken breast filets
1 cup rice
1 8-ounce jar
  mushrooms
1 can cream of
  mushroom soup
1 can cream of chicken
  soup
1 cup water
1 envelope dry onion
  soup mix

Rinse chicken and pat dry. Arrange in buttered 9x13-inch baking pan. Combine rice, mushrooms, soups and water in bowl; mix well. Pour over chicken. Sprinkle with dry onion soup mix. Bake, covered with foil at 375 degrees for 1 1/2 to 2 hours or until very tender. Yield: 8 servings.

Approx Per Serving: *Cal 363; Prot 30.3 g; Carbo 31.7 g; T Fat 12.5 g; Chol 75.5 mg; Potas 389.0 mg; Sod 1742.0 mg.*

Judy Frank
Ridgeland, South Carolina

CHICKEN GUISEPPE

This is good served with linguine with garlic butter sauce.

4 chicken breast filets
1/2 cup butter
4 slices provolone cheese
1 cup (or less) Marsala
1 12-ounce can
    mushrooms, drained
1/4 cup butter
2 tablespoons (about)
    flour

Rinse chicken and pat dry. Cook in 1/2 cup butter in skillet over medium-low heat for 15 to 20 minutes or until brown. Place in baking dish. Top with cheese. Bake at 350 degrees just until cheese melts. Add wine, mushrooms and 1/4 cup butter to pan drippings in skillet. Stir in flour gradually. Cook until thickened, stirring constantly. Spoon sauce over chicken. Yield: 4 servings.

Approx Per Serving: *Cal 596; Prot 31.3 g; Carbo 7.9 g; T Fat 45.2 g; Chol 175.0 mg; Potas 389.0 mg; Sod 838.0 mg.*

Peter R. Sarra
Canton, Massachusetts

CHICKEN JAMBALAYA with Creole Sauce

Serve this topped with Creole Sauce and hot sourdough French bread. I prefer Tasso or Cure 81 for the smoked ham.

1 3-pound chicken,
    cooked
2 bay leaves
1 teaspoon garlic powder
1/2 teaspoon cayenne
    pepper
1 teaspoon white pepper
1 teaspoon salt
1 1/2 cups finely chopped
    onion
1 1/2 cups finely chopped
    green bell pepper
1 1/2 cups finely chopped
    celery
1/4 cup margarine
1/2 teaspoon Tabasco
    sauce
1 2/3 cups chopped
    smoked ham
3/4 cup tomato sauce
2 cups rice
3 cups chicken stock
Creole Sauce (page 95)

Bone chicken and chop into bite-sized pieces. Combine bay leaves, garlic powder, cayenne pepper, white pepper and salt in small bowl; set aside. Sauté half the onion, green pepper and celery in margarine in 4-quart saucepan. Stir in mixed seasonings, Tabasco sauce and ham. Sauté over high heat for 20 minutes or until onions are dark brown. Add remaining onion, green pepper and celery. Cook for 5 minutes, stirring constantly. Add tomato sauce. Simmer for 5 minutes, stirring constantly. Add chicken. Cook over high heat for 15 minutes, stirring occasionally. Stir in rice; reduce heat. Simmer for 12 minutes. Add chicken stock. Bring to a boil; reduce heat. Simmer for 15 minutes or until rice is tender but still firm. May add additional chicken stock if needed for desired consistency. Remove bay leaf. Yield: 4 servings.

Approx Per Serving: *Cal 983; Prot 73.8 g; Carbo 87.2 g; T Fat 35.6 g; Chol 188.0 mg; Potas 1300.0 mg; Sod 2413.0 mg.*

Creole Sauce

2 bay leaves
3/4 teaspoon oregano
1/2 teaspoon sweet
   paprika
1/2 teaspoon thyme
1/2 teaspoon sweet basil
1/2 teaspoon salt
1/2 teaspoon pepper
1/2 teaspoon white pepper
1/2 teaspoon cayenne
   pepper
1/4 cup unsalted butter
1 cup chopped peeled
   tomatoes
3/4 cup chopped onion
3/4 cup chopped green
   bell pepper
3/4 cup chopped celery
11/2 teaspoons minced
   garlic
11/4 cups chicken stock
1 cup tomato sauce
1 teaspoon sugar
1/2 teaspoon Tabasco sauce

Mix bay leaves, oregano, paprika, thyme, basil, salt, pepper, white pepper and cayenne pepper in small bowl. Melt butter in large skillet over medium heat. Stir in tomatoes, onion, green pepper and celery. Add garlic and seasoning mixture. Sauté for 5 minutes or until onion is transparent. Stir in chicken stock, tomato sauce, sugar and Tabasco sauce. Bring to a boil; reduce heat. Simmer for 20 minutes or until vegetables are tender, stirring occasionally. Remove bay leaves. Yield: 2 1/2 cups.

Approx Per Cup: *Cal 653; Prot 14.2 g; Carbo 46.9 g; T Fat 49.3 g; Chol 125.0 mg; Potas 2148.0 mg; Sod 3639.0 mg.*

Dona J. Kemper
Cheyenne, Wyoming

HAWAIIAN CHICKEN

2 pounds cut-up chicken
1   8-ounce can
   pineapple slices
1/3 cup steak sauce
2 tablespoons honey

Rinse chicken and pat dry. Place in baking dish. Season with salt and pepper to taste. Bake at 400 degrees for 30 minutes. Drain pineapple, reserving 2 tablespoons liquid. Combine reserved liquid with steak sauce and honey in small bowl; mix well. Pour over chicken. Bake for 25 minutes longer, basting occasionally. Place pineapple over chicken. Bake for 10 minutes longer. Skim sauce. Serve over chicken.
Yield: 4 servings.

Approx Per Serving: *Cal 419; Prot 50.0 g; Carbo 23.7 g; T Fat 12.7 g; Chol 152.0 mg; Potas 477.0 mg; Sod 147.0 mg.*

Audrey Hopkins
Fremont, Michigan

CHICKEN JUAN DE SHAWN

4 chicken breast filets
1/2 cup flour
3 tablespoons oil
1 cup Sherry
1 cup water
1 lemon, sliced

Rinse chicken and pat dry. Season with salt and pepper to taste. Coat with flour. Brown in oil in skillet. Add Sherry and water. Simmer, covered, for 20 to 25 minutes or until chicken is tender. Top with lemon slices. Let stand for 2 minutes. Serve with rice or noodles. Yield: 4 servings.

Approx Per Serving: *Cal 386; Prot 27.0 g; Carbo 12.7 g; T Fat 17.0 g; Chol 72.0 mg; Potas 268.0 mg; Sod 65.7 mg.*

Pamela Arena Weidel, Boxwood Farm
Pennington, New Jersey

CHICKEN KIEV

6 chicken breast filets
Rosemary to taste
Garlic powder to taste
6 tablespoons cold butter
2 cups bread crumbs
2 eggs, beaten
1 tablespoon water
Oil for deep frying

Rinse chicken and pat dry. Flatten with rolling pin. Season with rosemary, garlic powder and salt and pepper to taste. Place 1 tablespoon butter in center of each piece of chicken. Roll to resemble drumstick, enclosing butter. Coat with bread crumbs. Dip into mixture of beaten eggs and water; roll in crumbs again. Repeat process, pressing crumbs to coat well. Place on waxed paper. Let stand for 20 to 30 minutes, turning chicken every 8 minutes or dry all surfaces. Heat oil to 300 degrees in electric skillet. Deep-fry chicken for 10 minutes or until brown. Insert frilled toothpick into 1 end. Arrange around bed of rice. Garnish with large sautéed mushroom and parsley bouquets. Yield: 6 servings.

Approx Per Serving: *Cal 425; Prot 31.8 g; Carbo 24.5 g; T Fat 21.6 g; Chol 196.0 mg; Potas 284.0 mg; Sod 425.0 mg.*
Nutritional information does not include oil for deep frying or rice.

Karen Spitzer
Temecula, California

KING RANCH CHICKEN

This popular Texas dish is really better the second day.

12 corn tortillas, cut up
1 can cream of
  mushroom soup
1 can cream of chicken
  soup
1 cup milk
1 cup chopped onion
1 cup chopped green bell
  pepper
2 4-ounce cans sliced
  mushrooms, drained
2 tablespoons chili powder
3 cups chopped cooked
  chicken
4 cups shredded sharp
  Cheddar cheese
1 10-ounce can Ro-Tel
  tomatoes

Line greased 3-quart baking dish with half the tortillas. Combine soups, milk, onion, green pepper, mushrooms and chili powder in bowl; mix well. Layer half the chicken, cheese and soup mixture in prepared dish. Repeat layers. Top with tomatoes. Bake at 350 degrees for 1 hour or until bubbly. Garnish with shredded lettuce and cherry tomato halves.
Yield: 10 servings.

Approx Per Serving: *Cal 459; Prot 29.1 g; Carbo 25.9 g; T Fat 26.8 g; Chol 91.2 mg; Potas 408.0 mg; Sod 975.0 mg.*

Marilyn Bevan, Bevan's Arabians
Rockwall, Texas

LEMON MINT CHICKEN

4 chicken breasts
1/4 cup fresh lemon juice
2 teaspoons chopped
  fresh mint
3 cloves of garlic, crushed
1 cup plain yogurt
1 teaspoon salt
1/4 teaspoon (or less) red
  pepper

Rinse chicken and pat dry. Combine lemon juice, mint, garlic, yogurt, salt and red pepper in bowl. Add chicken. Marinate in refrigerator for 1 hour to overnight. Drain marinade. Grill over coals or broil in oven for 20 minutes or until tender. Yield: 4 servings.

Approx Per Serving: *Cal 209; Prot 27.5 g; Carbo 4.7 g; T Fat 8.5 g; Chol 79.4 mg; Potas 324.0 mg; Sod 619.0 mg.*

Don Miller
Shreveport, Louisiana

CHICKEN LINGUINE

4 whole boneless
  chicken breasts
2 tablespoons olive oil
2 medium onions, chopped
2 yellow bell peppers,
  chopped
1¹/₂ cups chopped celery
1 20-ounce can tomatoes
1¹/₂ cups sliced
  mushrooms
1¹/₂ cups chopped zucchini
1 or 2 pinches cayenne
  pepper
¹/₃ cup Parmesan cheese
1 pound linguine, cooked

Rinse chicken and pat dry. Cut into bite-sized pieces. Stir-fry in olive oil in wok or skillet. Push chicken to 1 side. Add onions, peppers, and celery. Stir-fry until tender-crisp. Add tomatoes, mushrooms and zucchini. Season with cayenne pepper and salt and pepper to taste. Sprinkle with Parmesan cheese. Cook until heated through. Serve over hot linguine. Garnish with additional Parmesan cheese. Yield: 8 servings.

Approx Per Serving: *Cal 466; Prot 35.9 g; Carbo 52.2 g; T Fat 12.2 g; Chol 74.6 mg; Potas 777.0 mg; Sod 261.0 mg.*

Linda K. Lervick
Stanwood, Washington

MEXICAN-STYLE CHICKEN

This special party dish is from New Mexico.

6 chicken breast filets
4 eggs
5 tablespoons taco sauce
¹/₄ teaspoon salt
2 cups fine dry bread
  crumbs
2 teaspoons chili powder
2 teaspoons cumin
¹/₂ teaspoon oregano
1¹/₂ teaspoons garlic salt
¹/₄ cup butter
4 cups shredded lettuce
1 cup sour cream
6 tablespoons thinly
  sliced green onions
12 cherry tomatoes
1 avocado, sliced
2 limes, cut into wedges

Rinse chicken and pat dry. Combine eggs, taco sauce and salt in bowl; mix well. Mix bread crumbs, chili powder, cumin, oregano and garlic salt in bowl. Dip chicken into egg mixture; coat well with crumbs. Melt butter in shallow baking dish in 375-degree oven. Place chicken in prepared dish, turning to coat well with butter. Bake for 35 minutes. Serve on bed of lettuce with sour cream, green onions, cherry tomatoes, avocado and lime wedges. Pass additional sour cream and salsa. Yield: 6 servings.

Approx Per Serving: *Cal 573; Prot 36.7 g; Carbo 32.6 g; T Fat 33.1 g; Chol 294.0 mg; Potas 738.0 mg; Sod 1135.0 mg.*

Mrs. Robert Kennaugh, Manx Farms
Corsicana, Texas

PEACHY CHICKEN CARINOSA

The men of my family always request this for birthday dinners.

4 whole chicken breasts
2 tablespoons oil
1 small onion, chopped
10 fresh mushrooms, sliced
1 7-ounce can water
  chestnuts, drained
1 can cream of chicken
  soup
1 can cream of
  mushroom soup
1/2 teaspoon poultry
  seasoning
1 20-ounce can peach
  halves

Rinse chicken and pat dry. Brown in oil in skillet. Remove to 3-quart baking dish. Sauté onion and mushrooms in pan drippings in skillet. Add water chestnuts and soups. Stir in poultry seasoning. Pour over chicken. Bake at 350 degrees for 50 minutes. Top with peach halves. Bake for 10 minutes longer. Yield: 4 servings.

Approx Per Serving: *Cal 689; Prot 55.8 g; Carbo 48.9 g; T Fat 30.6 g; Chol 151.0 mg; Potas 822.0 mg; Sod 1350.0 mg.*

Ruth Husband
Brea, California

PHUDPUCKER'S CLUCKER

This dish should be served as soon as it comes from the oven.

8 chicken breast filets
4 green onions, sliced
1/2 teaspoon tarragon
2 tablespoons butter
3/4 cup dry white wine
1 egg white
2/3 cup mayonnaise
1/4 cup Parmesan cheese

Rinse chicken and pat dry. Arrange in 9x13-inch baking dish. Sprinkle with green onions and tarragon. Dot with butter. Add wine. Bake at 350 degrees for 30 minutes. Beat egg white in bowl until stiff peaks form. Fold in mayonnaise. Spoon evenly over chicken. Top with cheese. Bake for 12 to 15 minutes longer or until light brown. Yield: 8 servings.

Approx Per Serving: *Cal 356; Prot 27.4 g; Carbo 1.0 g; T Fat 24.8 g; Chol 90.5 mg; Potas 251.0 mg; Sod 222.0 mg.*

Ginger Detterman
Thousand Oaks, California

CHICKEN BREASTS POACHED IN ONION SOUP

4 chicken breast filets
1 envelope dry onion
  soup mix
1 chicken bouillon cube
2/3 cup flour
3/4 cup water
1 8-ounce package
  noodles, cooked

Rinse chicken; pat dry. Prepare soup according to package directions adding bouillon cube. Bring to a boil. Add chicken. Simmer for 6 minutes; remove from heat. Let stand for 20 minutes. Remove chicken. Bring cooking liquid to a boil. Stir in mixture of flour and water. Cook until thickened, stirring constantly. Add chicken. Heat to serving temperature. Serve over noodles. Yield: 4 servings.

Approx Per Serving: *Cal 515; Prot 37.3 g; Carbo 70.8 g; T Fat 8.8 g; Chol 72.0 mg; Potas 543.0 mg; Sod 2254.0 mg.*

Dottie Weaver, Shifting Sands Ranch
Bicknell, Utah

SESAME CHICKEN

This recipe is originally from The Silver Palate food shop in New York.

3 pounds cut-up chicken
1 teaspoon Italian
  seasoning
1 teaspoon tarragon
1 cup buttermilk
1 cup unseasoned dry
  bread crumbs
3/4 cup toasted sesame
  seed
1/3 cup chopped parsley
1/4 cup melted butter

Rinse chicken and pat dry. Place in glass dish. Sprinkle with Italian seasoning, tarragon and salt and pepper to taste. Pour buttermilk over top. Marinate for 2 hours or longer. Mix bread crumbs, sesame seed and parsley in small bowl. Drain chicken; coat with crumb mixture. Arrange in baking dish. Drizzle with melted butter. Bake at 350 degrees for 40 to 45 minutes or until tender. Serve hot or at room temperature. Yield: 6 servings.

Approx Per Serving: *Cal 474; Prot 52.9 g; Carbo 14.4 g; T Fat 21.5 g; Chol 175.0 mg; Potas 520.0 mg; Sod 377.0 mg.*

Diane Fortuna
Santa Barbara, California

SWISS CHICKEN AND HAM BAKE

1/2 cup chopped onion
2 tablespoons butter
3 tablespoons flour
1/2 teaspoon salt
1/4 teaspoon pepper
1 3-ounce can sliced
   mushrooms
1 cup light cream
2 tablespoons dry Sherry
2 cups chopped cooked
   chicken
1 cup chopped cooked ham
1 5-ounce can sliced
   water chestnuts
1/2 cup shredded Swiss
   cheese
1 1/2 cups soft bread crumbs
3 tablespoons melted
   butter

Sauté onion in 2 tablespoons butter in saucepan. Stir in flour, salt and pepper. Add undrained mushrooms, cream and Sherry. Cook until thickened, stirring constantly. Stir in chicken, ham and drained water chestnuts. Spoon into 1 1/2-quart baking dish. Top with cheese. Sprinkle mixture of bread crumbs and 3 tablespoons melted butter around edge. Bake at 400 degrees for 25 minutes or until light brown. Yield: 6 servings.

Approx Per Serving: *Cal 452; Prot 24.2 g; Carbo 14.7 g; T Fat 32.4 g; Chol 135.0 mg; Potas 319.0 mg; Sod 734.0 mg.*

Debby Cain
Oregon, Illinois

TURKEY AND HOT PASTA SALAD

I never use recipes so a friend watched me make this and wrote down what I did.

20 dried Chinese
   mushrooms
1 red bell pepper
1 green bell pepper
2 cups chopped smoked
   turkey
4 ounces feta cheese
1/3 cup capers
Juice of 1/4 lemon
1/2 cup mayonnaise
8 ounces spiral pasta,
   cooked

Rehydrate mushrooms according to package directions. Cut peppers into julienne strips. Combine mushrooms, peppers, turkey, cheese, capers, lemon juice and mayonnaise in bowl; mix well. Add pasta and salt and pepper to taste. Spoon into baking dish. Bake at 350 degrees for 25 to 30 minutes or until bubbly. Yield: 6 servings.

Approx Per Serving: *Cal 446; Prot 23.1 g; Carbo 41.1 g; T Fat 21.8 g; Chol 63.1 mg; Potas 309.0 mg; Sod 351.0 mg.*

T. G. Cyn
Gainesville, Virginia

Cantering To The Cove

TOLLARD PARK EGGS WITH SALMON

*Serve this with very thinly sliced brown bread and butter
and a bottle of Dom Perignon '82.*

Eggs, beaten
Butter
Smoked salmon, finely
   chopped
Aspic or consommé

Scramble eggs in butter in skillet until soft-set. Let stand until cool. Add salmon; mix gently. Spoon into crystal serving bowl. Pour a layer of aspic carefully over top. Chill until set.

Nutritional information is not available.

 William Davis, King John's House
Tollard Royal, England

EGGS AND CRAB MEAT LYONS

The Egg...what a wonderful work of nature it is...to be turned into a custard, a soufflé, an omelet, or a shampoo. No lunch in France starts without eggs in some form or other...a cold dish in summer...a hot one in winter. Never mind the cholesterol.

6 hard-boiled eggs
1 pound fresh crab meat
2 tablespoons (or more) Sherry
3 cups white sauce
1 tablespoon chopped fresh parsley
1 tablespoon chopped fresh dill
3 tablespoons buttered bread crumbs
2 tablespoons butter

Cut eggs into halves; arrange in buttered oven-proof serving dish. Sprinkle crab meat over eggs. Drizzle with Sherry. Spread with white sauce. Sprinkle with parsley and dill. Top with buttered bread crumbs; dot with butter. Bake at 350 degrees just until light brown. Voila! Quick and easy. Yield: 4 servings.

Approx Per Serving: *Cal 493; Prot 40.2 g; Carbo 20.2 g; T Fat 26.1 g; Chol 566.0 mg; Potas 817.0 mg; Sod 1101.0 mg.*

 Mrs. William Randolph Hearst, Jr.
New York, New York

ARABIAN SIKH SAMAK

This is an Arabian recipe for fish kabobs. Serve with a summer salad.

2 pounds swordfish
1 large onion, finely chopped
2 bay leaves, crumbled
1/2 cup olive oil
1/4 cup lemon juice
Peppercorns to taste
1 cup chopped flat-leaf parsley
1 lemon, sliced
1 green bell pepper, cut into pieces
8 mushrooms
2 stalks celery, cut into pieces
2 tomatoes, cut into large wedges

Wash fish and pat dry. Cut into 1-inch cubes. Layer fish, onion and bay leaves in dish. Pour olive oil and lemon juice over layers. Sprinkle with salt to taste, peppercorns and parsley. Top with lemon slices. Marinate for 2 hours. Drain. Alternate fish with vegetables on skewers. Grill over medium coals until fish flakes easily, turning occasionally. Yield: 4 servings.

Nutritional information is not available.

Excerpted from **Aramco World**

BAKED FISH SPANISH-STYLE

2 tablespoons oil
2 large onions
2 tablespoons chopped
  pimento
2 pounds 1½-inch thick
  halibut
½ teaspoon red pepper
1 teaspoon salt
Freshly ground pepper
4 thick tomato slices
3 tablespoons chopped
  chives
8 ounces mushrooms
¼ cup oil
1 teaspoon
  Worcestershire sauce
¾ cup bread crumbs

Spread 2 tablespoons oil over bottom of oven-proof serving dish. Thinly slice onions. Layer onions and pimento in dish. Wash fish and pat dry. Cut into 4 portions. Sprinkle with mixture of red pepper, salt and freshly ground pepper to taste. Arrange in prepared dish. Top with tomato slices. Sprinkle with chives and sliced mushrooms. Heat ¼ cup oil with Worcestershire sauce in small skillet. Add bread crumbs. Sauté until brown. Sprinkle over fish. Bake at 350 degrees for 35 to 40 minutes or just until fish flakes easily. Serve at once. Yield: 4 servings.

Approx Per Serving: *Cal 550; Prot 52.0 g; Carbo 23.4 g; T Fat 27.1 g; Chol 73.5 mg; Potas 1441.0 mg; Sod 811.0 mg.*

Ruth Husband
Brea, California

FILLETS OF SOLE BONNE FEMME

2 shallots, chopped
2 tablespoons butter
2½ pounds sole fillets
8 mushrooms, sliced
½ teaspoon salt
⅛ teaspoon pepper
1 cup dry white wine
1 tablespoon chopped
  parsley
2 tablespoons butter
1½ tablespoons flour

Sauté shallots in 2 tablespoons butter in large skillet for 2 minutes. Wash fillets and pat dry. Arrange over shallots. Top with mushrooms. Sprinkle with salt and pepper. Add wine. Bring to a boil; reduce heat. Simmer, covered, for 10 minutes. Add parsley. Cook for 5 minutes longer or until fish flakes easily. Drain well, reserving 1 cup cooking liquid. Place fish and mushrooms in 8x12-inch baking dish. Melt 2 tablespoons butter in skillet. Stir in flour. Add reserved liquid gradually. Cook over medium heat until thickened, stirring constantly. Pour over fish. Broil for 3 to 5 minutes or until top is golden brown. Yield: 6 servings.

Approx Per Serving: *Cal 328; Prot 37.9 g; Carbo 14.7 g; T Fat 10.0 g; Chol 111.0 mg; Potas 985.0 mg; Sod 405.0 mg.*

Jennifer Jo Bird, Jen-Mar Arabians
Manor, Texas

TROUT ALMONDINE

We make this with trout we catch down the road at White's Mill, an old grist mill where you can still buy freshly ground cornmeal.

4 whole trout
1 cup melted butter
Paprika to taste
1 cup slivered almonds
Juice and grated rind of
   1 lemon

Wash trout inside and out and pat dry. Combine with just enough water to cover in electric skillet. Cook for 12 minutes. Remove carefully to shallow baking dish. Drizzle with melted butter. Sprinkle with paprika and salt and pepper to taste. Broil for 5 minutes, basting occasionally with butter. Sauté almonds in 1 tablespoon butter in skillet. Add lemon juice and lemon rind. Place fish on serving plate. Spoon almonds over top. Yield: 4 servings.

Approx Per Serving: *Cal 1080; Prot 83.0 g; Carbo 7.9 g; T Fat 80.0 g; Chol 501.0 mg; Potas 1823.0 mg; Sod 654.0 mg.*

Bliss Brown, Paramont Arabians
Abingdon, Virginia

BLACKENED TUNA

We sometimes serve this on green salad.

1 onion, chopped
1/2 green bell pepper,
   chopped
2 teaspoons low
   cholesterol margarine
1 6-ounce can tuna,
   drained
2 teaspoons (or less)
   Creole seasoning

Sauté onion and green pepper in margarine in skillet. Add shredded tuna and seasoning. Sauté until very brown. Yield: 3 servings.

Approx Per Serving: *Cal 157; Prot 17.3 g; Carbo 4.8 g; T Fat 7.4 g; Chol 10.0 mg; Potas 234.0 mg; Sod 232.0 mg.*

Judith F. Hess
Glendora, California

HONEY-FRIED WALLEYE FILLETS

Visitors to Heartland enjoy these fillets of walleye from the nearby Missouri River.

4 large walleye fillets
1 tablespoon honey
1 egg, slightly beaten
2 cups crushed butter
  crackers
1/4 cup flour
1/8 teaspoon nutmeg
1/2 teaspoon salt
1/4 teaspoon pepper
2/3 cup oil

Wash fillets and pat dry. Combine honey and egg in bowl; mix well. Mix cracker crumbs, flour, nutmeg, salt and pepper in bowl. Dip fish in egg mixture; coat with crumbs. Fry in oil in skillet for 3 minutes on each side or until golden brown. Yield: 6 servings.

Approx Per Serving: *Cal 502; Prot 24.6 g; Carbo 27.0 g; T Fat 35.9 g; Chol 93.3 mg; Potas 366.0 mg; Sod 555.0 mg.*

Jayne D. Solberg, Heartland Farms
Baltic, South Dakota

AVOCADO CRAB MORNAY

1/4 cup melted butter
1/4 cup flour
1 cup light cream
1/2 cup chicken broth
1/2 cup Sherry
1/4 cup Parmesan cheese
2 tablespoons shredded
  Swiss cheese
1/8 teaspoon nutmeg
1/4 teaspoon salt
1/8 teaspoon pepper
6 scallions, sliced
1/4 cup butter
3 avocados, chopped
1 1/2 pounds crab meat

Blend 1/4 cup butter and flour in saucepan. Add cream and chicken broth. Cook until thickened, stirring until smooth. Blend in Sherry, cheeses and seasonings; remove from heat. Sauté scallions in 1/4 cup butter in skillet until tender-crisp. Add to sauce. Cook until heated through, stirring gently; do not boil. Fold in avocados and crab meat. Mound crab meat mixture into scallop shells. Bake at 500 degrees for 5 minutes. Garnish with additional Parmesan cheese. Serve immediately. Yield: 8 servings.

Approx Per Serving: *Cal 498; Prot 23.7 g; Carbo 18.8 g; T Fat 36.0 g; Chol 155.0 mg; Potas 980.0 mg; Sod 527.0 mg.*

Mona Schlageter
San Luis Obispo, California

DEVILED CRAB CALIFORNIA

I serve this dish with sourdough bread and fresh spinach salad.
It is also good served in scallop shells as a luncheon dish.

1¹/₂ teaspoons dry mustard
¹/₈ teaspoon Tabasco sauce
1 teaspoon
  Worcestershire sauce
¹/₂ cup dry Sherry
2 tablespoons fresh
  lemon juice
2 tablespoons chopped
  fresh parsley
³/₄ cup finely chopped
  onion
¹/₂ cup finely chopped
  celery
3 tablespoons butter
1 tablespoon oil
3 tablespoons flour
1¹/₂ cups milk
1 cup light cream
3 hard-boiled eggs
1 pound crab meat
¹/₂ cup Parmesan cheese
White pepper to taste
1 tablespoon butter
Paprika to taste

Mix dry mustard, Tabasco sauce, Worcestershire sauce, Sherry, lemon juice and parsley in bowl; set aside. Sauté onion and celery in 3 tablespoons butter and oil in skillet. Stir in flour gradually. Cook for 3 to 4 minutes, stirring constantly. Heat milk and cream just to the simmering point in small saucepan. Add milk and seasoning mixture to skillet. Cook for 3 to 4 minutes or until thickened, stirring constantly. Chop eggs and flake crab meat. Stir into sauce. Season with salt and white pepper to taste. Spoon into 8x11-inch baking dish. Sprinkle with cheese; dot with 1 tablespoon butter. Sprinkle with paprika. Bake at 375 degrees for 15 minutes or until light brown. Yield: 6 servings.

Approx Per Serving: *Cal 438; Prot 24.9 g; Carbo 10.4 g; T Fat 30.6 g; Chol 291.0 mg; Potas 506.0 mg; Sod 495.0 mg.*

Betty West
Temecula, California

DELICIOUS FLORIDA SHRIMP

We get our shrimp and oysters from beautiful Cedar Key.

2 pounds fresh large
  shrimp
¹/₂ cup butter
1 teaspoon (about) garlic
  powder
Juice of 1 lemon

Peel, vein and rinse shrimp. Sauté in butter in skillet over medium-low heat just until pink and opaque. Do not overcook. Sprinkle with garlic powder and lemon juice. Cook for 1 minute longer. Yield: 4 servings.

Approx Per Serving: *Cal 438; Prot 47.9 g; Carbo 3.2 g; T Fat 25.5 g; Chol 504.0 mg; Potas 466.0 mg; Sod 702.0 mg.*

Jackie Ivines
Trenton, Florida

EASY EASY SHRIMP CREOLE

This dish is always better the next day. We serve it with steamed green beans or Cajun green beans and garlic French bread.

1 medium onion, chopped
1 small green bell pepper, chopped
2 tablespoons olive oil
1   8-ounce can tomato sauce
1   10-ounce can Ro-Tel tomatoes
1 teaspoon minced garlic
1 pound shrimp, peeled

Sauté onion and green pepper in olive oil in skillet. Add tomato sauce, Ro-Tel tomatoes, garlic and pepper to taste. Simmer until heated through. Add shrimp. Simmer until shrimp are tender. Serve over rice. Yield: 3 servings.

Approx Per Serving: *Cal 300; Prot 34.6 g; Carbo 15.8 g; T Fat 11.3 g; Chol 295.0 mg; Potas 922.0 mg; Sod 952.0 mg.*

Steve and Rebecca Galloway
Lexington, Kentucky

108

SHRIMP SAUCE

Laissez les bons temps rouler! or Let the good times roll.

1/4 cup unsalted butter
1/3 cup light olive oil
1/2 cup flour
1/3 cup finely chopped
   parsley
1/3 cup chopped onion
6 Ro-Tel tomatoes,
   chopped
1 teaspoon allspice
1 tablespoon basil
1/2 teaspoon rosemary
1/8 teaspoon salt
1/2 teaspoon white pepper
3/4 pound peeled shrimp
15 medium mushrooms,
   thickly sliced
4 tablespoons Meyers Rum

Combine butter, olive oil and flour in saucepan. Cook over medium heat until peanut-butter color, stirring constantly. Add parsley, onion, tomatoes, allspice, basil, rosemary, salt and pepper. Simmer for 15 to 20 minutes. Add shrimp and mushrooms. Cook over medium heat for 5 to 8 minutes, stirring constantly. Stir in rum. Cook for 5 minutes longer or just until shrimp are tender. Yield: 6 servings.

Approx Per Serving: *Cal 300; Prot 14.5 g; Carbo 15.3 g; T Fat 20.7 g; Chol 131.3 mg; Potas 453.7 mg; Sod 187.0 mg.*

Phil Witter, Live Oak Arabians
Baton Rouge, Louisiana

LOUISIANA SHRIMP AND BUTTER BEANS

Serve over rice with crusty French bread. The tomato adds the perfect touch of color to this dish.

1 medium onion
1 medium tomato, peeled
2 small stalks celery
2 cloves of garlic
3 tablespoons safflower
   oil
2 tablespoons flour
2 cups butter beans
2 1/2 cups peeled shrimp
2 green onions with tops,
   chopped
3 tablespoons chopped
   parsley

Chop onion, tomato, celery and garlic. Blend oil and flour in saucepan. Cook until light brown, stirring constantly. Add butter beans and onion. Cook over low heat for several minutes, stirring constantly. Add tomato, celery and garlic. Cook for several minutes. Add shrimp. Cook until shrimp are pink. Add green onions and water to cover. Simmer until beans are tender. Stir in parsley and salt and red pepper to taste. Yield: 4 servings.

Approx Per Serving: *Cal 578; Prot 50.6 g; Carbo 66.6 g; T Fat 12.7 g; Chol 276.0 mg; Potas 2066.0 mg; Sod 357.0 mg.*

Don Miller
Shreveport, Louisiana

MARGEE'S SHRIMP

My best friend Margee brought this recipe to me on one of her visits. We serve it with crisp salad, lots of fresh French bread and steamed washcloths.

1 pound butter
1/4 cup Worcestershire
   sauce
1/2 teaspoon garlic
   powder
1/2 teaspoon thyme
1 tablespoon salt
2 tablespoons (or less)
   cayenne pepper
1 tablespoon pepper
3 pounds shrimp in shell

Melt butter in 9x13-inch baking pan. Stir in Worcestershire sauce, garlic powder, thyme, salt, cayenne pepper and pepper. Add shrimp with shells; stir to coat well. Marinate at room temperature for 1 hour, stirring several times. Bake at 375 degrees for 30 to 45 minutes or until pink. Yield: 4 servings.

Nutritional information is not available.

Bob and Judy Harvey
Lake Geneva, Wisconsin

SHRIMP SCAMPI

Okies don't eat much shrimp, but since my brother-in-law owns the New England Shrimp Company, we eat shrimp at our house any time he sends them.

1/4 cup virgin olive oil
2 cloves of garlic, crushed
1/4 cup lemon juice
2 shallots, finely chopped
2 pounds peeled shrimp
2 cloves of garlic, crushed
Butter

Combine olive oil, 2 cloves of garlic, lemon juice and shallots in bowl; mix well. Add salt and pepper to taste. Add shrimp. Sauté 2 cloves of garlic in desired amount of butter in skillet. Add shrimp mixture. Cook until shrimp are pink. Reduce heat. Cook, covered, for 5 to 8 minutes or to desired consistency. Serve over hot cooked rice. Yield: 4 servings.

Approx Per Serving: *Cal 380; Prot 48.7 g; Carbo 8.7 g; T Fat 16.0 g; Chol 442.0 mg; Potas 572.0 mg; Sod 516.0 mg.*
Nutritional information does not include butter.

Dr. Bill Pickett, Colorado State University
Fort Collins, Colorado

Something On The Side

Vegetables and Side Dishes

TRACY BLAKE'S LETTUCE SOUFFLÉ

Mr. and Mrs. Brian Blake are owners of a large Arab stud farm outside Manchester, England. Their home is Blyth House where Noel Coward wrote "Blyth Spirit."

1 small onion, finely
  chopped
2 tablespoons butter
8 ounces iceberg lettuce,
  chopped
1/4 cup butter
3 tablespoons flour
1/2 cup milk
4 ounces Gruyère cheese
4 egg yolks
4 egg whites, stiffly
  beaten

Sauté onion in 2 tablespoons butter in skillet until tender. Cook lettuce in a small amount of water in saucepan just until tender; drain. Add 1 tablespoon butter. Cook until remaining water evaporates, stirring frequently. Melt remaining 3 tablespoons butter in medium saucepan. Blend in flour and salt and pepper to taste. Cook for 3 to 5 minutes, stirring constantly. Stir in milk. Cook until thickened, stirring constantly; remove from heat. Stir in cheese until melted. Stir a small amount of hot mixture into egg yolks; stir egg yolks into hot mixture. Stir in onion and lettuce. Fold stiffly beaten egg whites into lettuce mixture. Pour into buttered 2-quart casserole. Bake at 375 degrees for 20 to 25 minutes or until well risen and golden brown. Yield: 6 servings.

Approx Per Serving: *Cal 273; Prot 11.6 g; Carbo 7.1 g; T Fat 22.1 g; Chol 237.0 mg; Potas 194.0 mg; Sod 218.0 mg.*

Mr. and Mrs. Brian Blake
Manchester, England

ARABIAN STUFFED GREEN PEPPERS

6 green bell peppers
3/4 cup pine nuts
4 large onions, chopped
1 1/2 cups olive oil
2 1/3 cups uncooked rice
1/2 cup currants
1 teaspoon salt
1 teaspoon pepper
1 tablespoon sugar
1/2 cup chopped mint
1 teaspoon allspice
2 tablespoons lemon
  juice
6 tomato slices
1 cup water

Slice stem ends from green peppers; remove membranes and seed. Sauté pine nuts and onions in olive oil. Add rice. Sauté for 5 minutes. Stir in currants, salt, pepper and sugar. Pour in water to 2 times depth of rice mixture. Simmer until water is absorbed, stirring frequently. Add mint, allspice and lemon juice. Spoon loosely into peppers. Top with tomato slices. Place stuffed peppers upright in large saucepan. Sprinkle with additional salt and sugar if desired. Drizzle with additional olive oil. Pour 1 cup water into pan. Simmer just until peppers are tender. Chill in refrigerator. Garnish with chopped fresh parsley, lemon slices and tomato wedges. Yield: 6 servings.

Nutritional information is not available.

*Excerpted from **Aramco World***

BARBECUED BEANS

This recipe is always the highlight of a picnic or buffet supper. It is wonderful with brisket, coleslaw and cheese grits. The original recipe came from Katy DeLine.

2 pounds Italian sausage
1   15-ounce can wax beans
1   15-ounce can green
    beans
1   15-ounce can pinto
    beans
1   15-ounce can baby
    lima beans
1   15-ounce can kidney
    beans
1   30-ounce can chili
    beans
1 can tomato soup
1   12-ounce can tomato
    paste
1 cup packed brown sugar
1   18-ounce jar plain
    barbecue sauce
1   18-ounce jar hot
    barbecue sauce

Crumble sausage into large skillet. Sauté until brown; drain. Drain canned wax, green, pinto, lima and kidney beans well. Stir in drained beans, chili beans, tomato soup, tomato paste, brown sugar and barbecue sauces. Pour into large casserole. Bake at 350 degrees for 1 hour or longer until flavors are blended.
Yield: 30 servings.

Approx Per Serving: *Cal 139; Prot 5.6 g; Carbo 27.7 g; T Fat 1.4 g; Chol 0.0 mg; Potas 449.0 mg; Sod 611.0 mg.*

Dotty Van Vleet
Denver, Colorado

RED BEANS AND RICE

Serve this over rice with garlic French bread on the side. This dish freezes very well.

1 pound dried red
    kidney beans
1 pound hot pork
    sausage, sliced
1 onion, finely chopped
1 teaspoon (or more) garlic
1/2 teaspoon cayenne
    pepper

Soak beans according to package directions; drain. Place in black iron pot with water to half the depth of beans. Add sausage, onion, garlic, pepper and salt to taste. Simmer, covered, for 2 hours or until beans are tender, stirring occasionally. Mash beans against side of pot with back of spoon to thicken. Add water if necessary. Simmer for 1 hour longer, stirring occasionally. Yield: 15 servings.

Approx Per Serving: *Cal 231; Prot 10.8 g; Carbo 19.3 g; T Fat 12.5 g; Chol 20.7 mg; Potas 506.0 mg; Sod 209.0 mg.*

Steve and Rebecca Galloway
Lexington, Kentucky

COWBOY BEANS

1¹/₂ pounds ground beef
¹/₂ pound bacon
1 cup chopped onion
1 32-ounce can pork and beans
1 16-ounce can kidney beans
1 16-ounce can butter beans
1¹/₂ cups catsup
¹/₂ cup packed brown sugar
1 tablespoon liquid smoke
3 tablespoons white vinegar
1 teaspoon salt
¹/₂ teaspoon pepper

Brown ground beef in skillet, stirring until crumbly; drain. Pour into 4-quart heavy saucepan. Chop bacon finely. Brown bacon and onion in skillet, stirring frequently; drain. Add to ground beef. Add pork and beans, kidney beans and butter beans; mix well. Stir in catsup, brown sugar, liquid smoke, vinegar, salt and pepper. Simmer, covered, for 1 hour or longer, stirring frequently. This recipe can be reduced or doubled. We like it with corn bread and fruit salad. Yield: 10 servings.

Approx Per Serving: *Cal 544; Prot 29.0 g; Carbo 56.7 g; T Fat 23.3 g; Chol 69.0 mg; Potas 929.0 mg; Sod 1616.0 mg.*

Joan Reno
Bucyrus, Kansas

SPICY BEAN BAKE

1 40-ounce can baked beans
1 16-ounce can red kidney beans
2 large apples, chopped
¹/₂ cup raisins
1¹/₂ cups chopped onions
1 cup chopped green bell pepper
3 cups chopped ham
4 slices crisp-fried bacon, crumbled
1 cup catsup
¹/₂ cup sweet pickle relish
¹/₂ cup packed brown sugar
1 teaspoon dry mustard
¹/₂ cup molasses

Combine beans, kidney beans, apples, raisins, onions, green pepper, ham and bacon in 3-quart casserole; mix well. Stir in catsup, pickle relish, brown sugar, mustard and molasses. Bake, covered, at 250 degrees for 1 hour and 30 minutes, stirring occasionally. May substitute cooked pork or beef for ham. Yield: 12 servings.

Approx Per Serving: *Cal 350; Prot 16.0 g; Carbo 61.9 g; T Fat 5.8 g; Chol 22.4 mg; Potas 863.0 mg; Sod 1172.0 mg.*

Joanne C. Triplett
Tucson, Arizona

SANTA MARIA BARBECUE BEANS

This is a central California coast recipe, made from locally grown "Poquito beans" and served with beef and salsa at the "Vanquero Rodeos" or cattle roundups. Each ranch has its subtle variation. This is mine.

2 pounds Poquito beans
3 tablespoons salt
1¹/₂ teaspoons pepper
1   1¹/₄-ounce envelope
   chili seasoning mix
¹/₂ pound bacon
3 cloves of garlic, minced
1 onion, finely chopped
¹/₂ pound ground beef
¹/₂ teaspoon oregano
¹/₂ teaspoon MSG
1¹/₂ cups tomato sauce
1   6-ounce can tomato
   paste
1   28-ounce can
   tomatoes, undrained

Rinse beans several times; drain. Place in large saucepan with water to cover. Add salt and pepper. Simmer for 2 hours, stirring occasionally. Stir in chili mix. Chop bacon finely. Sauté garlic, onion, ground beef and bacon in skillet until ground beef is brown and crumbly, stirring frequently; drain. Add ground beef mixture, oregano, MSG, tomato sauce, tomato paste and tomatoes to beans. Simmer for 1 hour longer or until beans are tender. Serve with salsa. May substitute ¹/₄ cup chili powder, 1 tablespoon oregano, 1 teaspoon cumin and any good Mexican spice for chili mix. Yield: 30 servings.

Approx Per Serving: *Cal 117; Prot 6.8 g; Carbo 11.5 g; T Fat 5.2 g; Chol 11.2 mg; Potas 362.0 mg; Sod 958.0 mg.*
Nutritional information does not include chili seasoning mix.

Don Severa
Templeton, California

CAJUN GREEN BEANS

This is a real favorite at a barbecue.

1 medium onion
¹/₂ green bell pepper
¹/₂ pound mushrooms
2 tablespoons butter
2   16-ounce cans French-
   style green beans,
   drained
1 can mushroom soup
1   6-ounce roll garlic
   cheese, shredded
¹/₂ teaspoon garlic
   powder
¹/₄ teaspoon white pepper

Chop onion and green pepper; slice mushrooms. Sauté onion, pepper and mushrooms in butter in large skillet until glazed. Add beans, soup and cheese. Simmer until cheese is melted, stirring frequently. Add garlic powder, white pepper and black pepper to taste; mix well. Spoon into 2-quart casserole. Bake at 350 degrees for 45 minutes to 1 hour. Yield: 6 servings.

Approx Per Serving: *Cal 230; Prot 9.1 g; Carbo 17.3 g; T Fat 14.9 g; Chol 28.9 mg; Potas 504.0 mg; Sod 1099.0 mg.*

Steve and Rebecca Galloway
Lexington, Kentucky

MARSH FAMILY FAVORITE BROCCOLI CASSEROLE

*This easy, make-ahead casserole is great and you don't see the
cottage cheese after it is cooked.*

1 10-ounce package
   frozen chopped broccoli
16 ounces cottage cheese
3 eggs, beaten
1/4 cup melted butter
1/4 cup flour
1 8-ounce package Old
   English cheese, cubed

Cook broccoli according to package directions; drain. Combine broccoli and cottage cheese in bowl; mix well. Stir in mixture of eggs, butter and flour. Add Old English cheese; mix well. Pour into 8-inch square baking dish. Bake at 300 degrees for 1 hour and 30 minutes or until lightly browned. Yield: 6 servings.

Approx Per Serving: *Cal 358; Prot 22.9 g; Carbo 9.4 g; T Fat 25.6 g; Chol 205.0 mg; Potas 250.0 mg; Sod 957.0 mg.*

Lisa Jo Marsh
Grand Blanc, Michigan

COPPER KETTLE CARROTS

2 cups shredded carrots
2 cups finely sliced
   green onions
1/4 cup butter
1/4 cup chicken broth
3/4 teaspoon fennel
3 tablespoons Grand
   Marnier

Stir-fry carrots and onions in butter in large skillet until onions are clear. Add chicken broth; mix well. Simmer, covered, just until carrots are tender. Add fennel. Stir in Grand Marnier just before serving. Garnish with chopped parsley. May substitute nutmeg or anise for fennel and Triple Sec or Cointreau for Grand Marnier. Yield: 6 servings.

Approx Per Serving: *Cal 125; Prot 1.2 g; Carbo 9.1 g; T Fat 7.9 g; Chol 20.7 mg; Potas 215.0 mg; Sod 111.0 mg.*

Mary Jane Parkinson
El Cajon, California

CRUNCHY SURPRISE CARROTS AND PEAS

I like vegetables and make my own recipes using them. This is very easy.

1 cup thinly sliced carrots
1 cup water
1 teaspoon salt
20 ounces frozen peas
1/4 cup maple syrup
1 8-ounce can sliced
   mushrooms, drained
1 8-ounce can sliced
   water chestnuts,
   drained
1/4 cup cornstarch

Combine carrots, water and salt in heavy 3-quart saucepan. Simmer, covered, for 5 minutes. Add peas. Simmer, covered, for 3 minutes. Add maple syrup, mushrooms and water chestnuts; mix well. Bring to a boil. Remove vegetables to serving dish. Stir cornstarch into remaining liquid. Cook for 1 minute or until thickened, stirring constantly. Pour over vegetables. Yield: 5 cups.

Approx Per Cup: *Cal 197; Prot 7.5 g; Carbo 42.5 g; T Fat 0.7 g; Chol 0.0 mg; Potas 372.0 mg; Sod 774.0 mg.*

R. Brown, Aristique Farms
Marion, Indiana

ORIENTAL CARROTS

This is an easy, make-ahead recipe.

1 can tomato soup
1/2 cup oil
1 cup (scant) sugar
1/2 cup vinegar
1 teaspoon (scant) salt
1/4 teaspoon pepper
1 teaspoon prepared
   mustard
5 cups sliced cooked
   carrots
1 medium onion, finely
   chopped
1 green bell pepper,
   finely chopped

Combine tomato soup, oil, sugar, vinegar, salt, pepper and mustard in saucepan. Simmer until sugar is dissolved, stirring constantly. Combine carrots, onion and green pepper in bowl; mix well. Pour tomato soup mixture over vegetables. Marinate, covered, overnight in refrigerator. May serve cold or hot. Yield: 6 servings.

Approx Per Serving: *Cal 397; Prot 2.7 g; Carbo 57.6 g; T Fat 19.3 g; Chol 0.0 mg; Potas 498.0 mg; Sod 797.0 mg.*

Jill S. Myles
Fort Collins, Colorado

GREEN CHILI CORN

This easy, make-ahead recipe freezes well. It is from my 5th and 6th grade "homeroom" teacher, Mulkey Gilliland.

8 ounces cream cheese
2 cups milk
2 teaspoons butter
3 16-ounce cans whole
   kernel corn, drained
1 4-ounce can green
   chilies, undrained
1 teaspoon salt
2 teaspoons pepper

Combine cream cheese, milk and butter in saucepan. Heat until blended, stirring constantly. Add corn, chilies, salt and pepper; mix well. Pour into 3-quart casserole. Bake at 350 degrees for 20 minutes or until golden brown. Yield: 8 servings.

Approx Per Serving: *Cal 289; Prot 8.9 g; Carbo 36.8 g; T Fat 14.6 g; Chol 41.8 mg; Potas 432.0 mg; Sod 779.0 mg.*

Gary L. Carpenter
Longmont, Colorado

ONIONS PARMESAN

These taste almost like noodles. Great with steak.

8 medium onions, sliced
1/4 cup butter
1/2 cup Parmesan cheese

Sauté onions in butter in skillet for 10 to 12 minutes. Place in 2½-quart baking dish. Sprinkle with cheese. Broil 5 inches from heat until cheese melts. Yield: 6 servings.

Approx Per Serving: *Cal 170; Prot 5.4 g; Carbo 15.9 g; T Fat 10.2 g; Chol 25.9 mg; Potas 340.0 mg; Sod 194.0 mg.*

Deedie Wrigley, Kaaba Arabian Enterprises
Scottsdale, Arizona

GRANDMA ELCOCK'S BEST PARSNIPS

Try this favorite recipe to accompany pork chops or steak.

1 pound parsnips, peeled
1/2 teaspoon salt
1 tablespoon butter
1 teaspoon dry mustard
1/3 cup packed brown
   sugar

Cut parsnips into 2-inch strips. Combine with salt and water to cover in saucepan. Simmer for 20 minutes or just until tender, stirring occasionally; drain. Add butter, mustard and brown sugar; mix well. Pour into serving dish. May double recipe, cook for several minutes longer and mash. Yield: 4 servings.

Approx Per Serving: *Cal 178; Prot 1.4 g; Carbo 37.9 g; T Fat 3.2 g; Chol 7.8 mg; Potas 489.0 mg; Sod 310.0 mg.*

Jo Ann Shea
St. Marys, Pennsylvania

EASY POTATOES

We have used this easy, make-ahead recipe for large groups and it is always well received. It is an old Pennsylvania-Czechoslovakian recipe.

**6 medium potatoes,
coarsely chopped
1 green bell pepper,
chopped
1 onion, chopped
1 tablespoon butter
1 tablespoon chopped
parsley
Paprika**

Place potatoes in saucepan with water to cover. Simmer just until potatoes are tender; drain. Sauté pepper and onion in butter in skillet until onion is soft. Add to potatoes; mix well. Add enough paprika to color and salt and pepper to taste. Serve immediately or if prepared ahead, microwave to reheat. Yield: 4 servings.

Approx Per Serving: *Cal 263; Prot 5.3 g; Carbo 54.7 g; T Fat 3.3 g; Chol 7.8 mg; Potas 1032.0 mg; Sod 38.4 mg.*

*Margaret D. Fleming, Traveler's Rest Arabians
Columbia, Tennessee*

GARLIC POTATOES

**6 medium potatoes,
coarsely chopped
2 cloves of garlic,
coarsely chopped
3 tablespoons olive oil**

Combine potatoes and garlic in bowl. Add oil; toss to coat. Microwave on High for 6 to 8 minutes. Place in single layer in oiled baking pan. Bake at 400 degrees for 45 minutes or until tender and brown. Yield: 4 servings.

Nutritional information is not available.

*Sylvia Rust
Willits, California*

119

POTATOES JURNEEKA

Jurneeka claimed that this recipe has been handed down from mother to daughter since great-great-great-great grandma Wadduda. (She told some tall tales!)

6 large potatoes
8 ounces sour cream
1 tablespoon garlic
  powder
2 teaspoons pepper
3 ounces bacon bits
2 ounces Cheddar
  cheese, shredded
Paprika

Place potatoes in skins on baking pan. Bake at 350 degrees for 1 hour and 30 minutes or until soft. Slice off top lengthwise. Scoop out potato with spoon, reserving shells. Combine pulp with sour cream, garlic powder and pepper in large mixer bowl. Beat until well blended and smooth. Stir in bacon bits. Spoon into reserved shells; sprinkle with cheese and dash of paprika for color. Place on baking sheet. Bake at 350 degrees for 20 minutes or until potatoes are hot and cheese is melting. Yield: 6 servings.

Approx Per Serving: *Cal 334; Prot 7.4 g; Carbo 41.3 g; T Fat 15.0 g; Chol 26.7 mg; Potas 698.0 mg; Sod 477.0 mg.*

B. Paul Husband
Saugus, California

MOTHER'S SHREDDED POTATOES

This is one of mother's recipes most loved by the family, known as Gramma's potatoes.

Potatoes
Onions
1/2 pound bacon
8 ounces sour cream
6 tablespoons butter
1 cup half and half

Wash desired number of potatoes. Shred as desired; place in saucepan with water to cover. Simmer until starch is cooked out. Drain; rinse. Shred onion as desired. Add to potatoes. Cook bacon in skillet until crisp; crumble. Add bacon and pan drippings to potatoes; mix well. Add sour cream, butter and half and half; mix well. Spoon into casserole. Bake, covered, at 325 degrees for 30 minutes.

Nutritional information is not available.

Crete B. Harvey
Stanwood, Washington

ZINGY POTATOES

This is an old Iowa farm recipe for spicing up mashed potatoes.
It goes great with roast beef and brown gravy.

9 medium potatoes
8 ounces cream cheese,
  softened
1 cup sour cream
1 teaspoon chopped
  chives
1 tablespoon butter

Peel potatoes; chop coarsely. Place in saucepan with salted water to cover. Simmer until tender; drain. Place in mixer bowl; beat until creamy. Add cream cheese and sour cream. Beat until well blended and fluffy. Season with chives and garlic salt to taste. Spoon into 2-quart casserole. Dot with butter; sprinkle with parsley flakes. Bake at 350 degrees for 30 minutes or until lightly browned. Yield: 6 servings.

Approx Per Serving: *Cal 448; Prot 8.6 g; Carbo 53.0 g; T Fat 23.4 g; Chol 63.4 mg; Potas 1016.0 mg; Sod 160.0 mg.*

Ron M. and Sandy Ballantine
Denver, Colorado

SQUASH DELIGHT

This recipe may be made a day ahead.

2 pounds green or
  yellow summer squash
2 eggs, beaten
1/4 cup melted butter
1 cup shredded sharp
  Cheddar cheese
1/4 cup melted butter
1 cup Melba toast crumbs

Wash and slice squash. Place in saucepan with a small amount of water and salt to taste. Simmer until tender; drain. Mash squash. Add eggs, 1/4 cup butter and cheese. Place in 2-quart casserole. Combine remaining butter and crumbs in bowl; mix well. Sprinkle over squash mixture. Bake at 300 degrees for 1 hour or until lightly browned. Garnish with additional cheese. Yield: 6 servings.

Approx Per Serving: *Cal 333; Prot 10.8 g; Carbo 19.2 g; T Fat 24.6 g; Chol 153.0 mg; Potas 365.0 mg; Sod 395.0 mg.*

Eloise B. Kline
Whittier, California

ZUCCHINI CASSEROLE

This has been my family's favorite casserole for years. The recipe has been duplicated and shared with numerous friends. Enjoy!

3 cups cooked sliced
  zucchini squash
1/2 cup sour cream
1 can cream of chicken
  soup
1 2-ounce jar chopped
  pimento
1 small onion, finely
  chopped
1/2 cup margarine
1 6-ounce package
  corn bread stuffing mix

Combine zucchini, sour cream, soup and pimento in bowl; mix well. Sauté onion in margarine in skillet until soft. Add both packages from stuffing mix; mix well. Alternate layers of zucchini mixture and stuffing in 1½-quart casserole, ending with stuffing. Bake at 350 degrees for 30 minutes or until hot and bubbly. Yield: 8 servings.

Approx Per Serving: *Cal 268; Prot 5.0 g; Carbo 23.6 g; T Fat 17.5 g; Chol 9.4 mg; Potas 255.0 mg; Sod 809.0 mg.*

Donna L. Jensen
Bradenton, Florida

EMPRESS ARABIANS ZUCCHINI SOUFFLÉ

3 eggs, beaten
1/2 cup oil
2 cups grated zucchini
1 cup shredded Cheddar
  cheese
1 small onion, grated
1/2 pound bacon, crisp-
  fried, crumbled
1 cup buttermilk baking
  mix

Combine eggs and oil in large bowl; mix well. Add zucchini, cheese, onion and bacon; mix well. Stir in baking mix. Pour into 9-inch square baking dish. Bake at 350 degrees for 40 minutes or until golden brown. Yield: 9 servings.

Approx Per Serving: *Cal 460; Prot 15.4 g; Carbo 21.3 g; T Fat 34.7 g; Chol 126.0 mg; Potas 296.0 mg; Sod 857.0 mg.*

Judy Frank
Ridgeland, South Carolina

1 pound mushrooms
1 small onion, grated
1/2 cup butter
1/4 cup flour
1 teaspoon salt
1/2 teaspoon pepper
1 teaspoon MSG
3 cups milk
12 ounces sharp Cheddar
  cheese, shredded
1/8 teaspoon hot pepper
  sauce
1 tablespoon soy sauce
1   10-ounce package
  frozen artichoke hearts
1   10-ounce package
  frozen green beans
1   10-ounce package
  frozen baby lima beans
1   7-ounce can water
  chestnuts
1/4 cup white wine
1   6-ounce can fried
  onion rings, crumbled

Slice mushrooms. Sauté mushrooms and onions in butter for 5 minutes or until lightly browned. Stir in mixture of flour, salt, pepper and MSG. Add milk. Simmer until thickened, stirring constantly. Add cheese, hot pepper sauce and soy sauce. Simmer until cheese is melted, stirring frequently. Cook artichoke hearts, green beans and lima beans according to package directions; drain. Add cooked vegetables, water chestnuts and wine to mushroom mixture. Toss lightly to mix. Pour into buttered 2-quart casserole. Bake at 350 degrees for 30 minutes. Sprinkle with crumbled onion rings. Bake for 10 minutes longer. Yield: 8 servings.

Approx Per Serving: *Cal 512; Prot 20.6 g; Carbo 34.7 g; T Fat 33.4 g; Chol 95.7 mg; Potas 727.0 mg; Sod 1412.0 mg.*

Jane L. Watson, Babson Arabian Horse Farm
Dixon, Illinois

ARABIAN CRACKED WHEAT

3 tablespoons butter or
  ghee
2 tablespoons cumin
4 red chili peppers
4 cups yogurt
1/2 teaspoon salt
4 cups cracked wheat
1/2 cup melted butter or
  ghee

Grind 3 tablespoons butter, cumin and chili peppers with mortar and pestle. Heat yogurt with salt over low heat to the boiling point, stirring constantly. Add butter mixture. Rinse and drain cracked wheat. Add to yogurt. Cook, covered, over low heat for 3 hours. Beat with wooden spoon or process in blender container. Pour into deep dish. Make hole in center. Pour in butter. Yield: 8 to 10 servings.

Nutritional information is not available.

*Excerpted from **Aramco World***

CORNY CORN MUFFIN CASSEROLE

This is an easy, make-ahead recipe with minimal preparation time and it is yummy.

1 16-ounce can cream-style corn
1 16-ounce can whole kernel corn
2 eggs, beaten
1/2 cup melted margarine
8 ounces sour cream
1 8 1/2-ounce package corn muffin mix

Combine cream-style corn, whole kernel corn, eggs, margarine and sour cream in bowl; mix well. Stir in muffin mix. Pour into greased 2-quart casserole. Bake at 350 degrees for 1 hour or until brown. Yield: 8 servings.

Approx Per Serving: *Cal 328; Prot 5.6 g; Carbo 33.0 g; T Fat 21.1 g; Chol 81.1 mg; Potas 240.0 mg; Sod 594.0 mg.*

Joanne C. Triplett
Tucson, Arizona

CHEESE GRITS CASSEROLE

This easy, make-ahead recipe is very good to serve with pork chops, chicken or barbecued brisket.

1 cup grits
3 cups boiling water
1/2 teaspoon salt
6 tablespoons margarine
8 ounces sharp Cheddar cheese, shredded
1 6-ounce roll jalapeño cheese, shredded
2 eggs, beaten
3 drops hot pepper sauce
Garlic

Cook grits in boiling water for 5 minutes, stirring frequently. Add salt and margarine; mix well. Add Cheddar cheese and jalapeño cheese; stir until melted. Stir in eggs, hot pepper sauce and desired amount of garlic. Pour into buttered 9-inch square baking dish. Bake at 250 degrees for 1 hour. Yield: 4 servings.

Approx Per Serving: *Cal 706; Prot 28.6 g; Carbo 35.8 g; T Fat 49.3 g; Chol 224.0 mg; Potas 306.0 mg; Sod 1264.0 mg.*

Dotty Van Vleet
Denver, Colorado

NOODLE PUDDING DELISH

8 ounces butter, softened
8 ounces cream cheese, softened
8 ounces sour cream
2 teaspoons vanilla extract
1 cup sugar
8 ounces fine noodles, cooked
1 cup slivered almonds

Process butter, cream cheese, sour cream, vanilla and sugar in blender container until smooth. Place noodles on bottom and sides of large buttered casserole. Pour butter mixture over noodles; do not mix. Sprinkle with almonds. Bake at 350 degrees for 1 hour. Yield: 6 servings.

Approx Per Serving: *Cal 884; Prot 13.5 g; Carbo 68.8 g; T Fat 63.9 g; Chol 141.0 mg; Potas 358.0 mg; Sod 394.0 mg.*

Gail Cohan, Dynasty Arabians II, Inc.
Delray Beach, Florida

SOUR CREAM NOODLES

This easy, make-ahead recipe is a favorite for our Thanksgiving and Christmas dinners.

1   16-ounce package noodles
1 cup cottage cheese
2 cups sour cream
1/4 cup finely chopped onion
1 clove of garlic, minced
2 teaspoons Worcestershire sauce
1/8 teaspoon hot pepper sauce
1 teaspoon salt
3 eggs, beaten
1/4 cup shredded Cheddar cheese
1/3 cup melted margarine

Cook noodles according to package directions to desired doneness. Place in 9x13-inch casserole. Combine cottage cheese, sour cream, onion, garlic, Worcestershire sauce, hot pepper sauce, salt, eggs and cheese in bowl; mix well. Pour over hot noodles. Drizzle margarine over top. Bake at 350 degrees for 1 hour. Garnish with sour cream and shredded cheese. Yield: 8 servings.

Approx Per Serving: *Cal 474; Prot 15.5 g; Carbo 46.9 g; T Fat 24.6 g; Chol 136.0 mg; Potas 281.0 mg; Sod 554.0 mg.*

Dotty Van Vleet
Denver, Colorado

PASTA CASSEROLE

2 large onions, chopped
8 ounces mushrooms,
  sliced
3/4 cup cottage cheese
8 ounces pasta, cooked
8 ounces sour cream
1 cup Parmesan cheese

Sauté onions in skillet until tender. Combine onions, mushrooms, cottage cheese and pasta in bowl; mix well. Reserve 2 tablespoons sour cream and 2 tablespoons Parmesan cheese. Add remaining sour cream and cheese to pasta mixture; mix well. Pour into 2-quart casserole. Bake at 325 degrees for 20 minutes. Spread reserved sour cream over top; sprinkle with reserved Parmesan cheese. Bake for 10 minutes longer. Yield: 8 servings.

Approx Per Serving: *Cal 252; Prot 12.2 g; Carbo 27.7 g; T Fat 10.4 g; Chol 23.3 mg; Potas 298.0 mg; Sod 286.0 mg.*

Crete B. Harvey
Stanwood, Washington

BARLEY PILAF

1/2 cup butter
13/4 cups pearl barley
2 cans beef broth
1 soup can water

Melt half the butter in heavy skillet. Pour in barley. Cook over low heat until golden brown, stirring frequently. Add remaining butter; stir until melted. Stir in beef broth and water. Pour into 2-quart casserole. Bake, covered, at 350 degrees for 45 minutes or until barley is tender, adding additional broth if necessary. May add toasted slivered almonds, mushrooms, shrimp, sausage, sliced hot dogs, leftover beef or chicken. Yield: 6 servings.

Approx Per Serving: *Cal 199; Prot 2.6 g; Carbo 12.9 g; T Fat 15.7 g; Chol 41.7 mg; Potas 77.1 mg; Sod 437.0 mg.*

Helen McCoy, McCoy Arabians
Chino Hills, California

RICE PILAF

3 cups rice
1/2 cup butter
6 cups beef broth

Sauté rice in butter in heavy skillet until butter begins to bubble. Pour into 1 1/2-quart casserole. Heat broth in skillet to the boiling point. Pour over rice. Add salt and pepper to taste; mix well. Bake at 375 degrees for 30 minutes. Stir until well mixed. Bake for 10 minutes longer. May substitute chicken broth for beef broth. Yield: 6 servings.

Approx Per Serving: *Cal 486; Prot 9.1 g; Carbo 74.6 g; T Fat 16.2 g; Chol 42.0 mg; Potas 220.0 mg; Sod 915.0 mg.*

Mrs. R. E. Newman
Morrison, Colorado

SPANISH RICE

1 cup rice
1 tablespoon oil
1 green bell pepper, chopped
1 small onion, chopped
1   8-ounce can tomatoes
1 cup water
1/2 teaspoon garlic powder
1/2 teaspoon cumin
1 teaspoon salt

Sauté rice in oil in large skillet until brown. Add green pepper and onion. Cook until brown, stirring frequently. Add tomatoes, water and seasonings. Simmer for 30 minutes or until rice is tender, stirring frequently. Yield: 4 servings.

Approx Per Serving: *Cal 230; Prot 4.4 g; Carbo 44.3 g; T Fat 4.0 g; Chol 0.0 mg; Potas 287.0 mg; Sod 630.0 mg.*

Rosalinda Reyes, Donoghue Arabian Farm
Goliad, Texas

TORTILLA CASSEROLE

This easy, make-ahead recipe can be frozen.

1 12-count package
   flour tortillas
1/3 cup shortening
1 cup finely chopped
   onion
2 tablespoons shortening
1 4-ounce can green
   chilies
1 cup whipping cream
1 cup tomato purée
8 ounces Monterey Jack
   cheese, shredded
2 tablespoons butter

Cut tortillas into thin strips. Cook in 1/3 cup shortening in skillet until crisp but not brown. Remove. Sauté onion in 2 tablespoons shortening in skillet until tender. Add green chilies, cream and tomato purée. Simmer for 10 minutes. Add salt to taste. Alternate layers of tortilla strips, tomato sauce and cheese in 2-quart buttered casserole, ending with cheese. Dot with butter. Bake at 350 degrees for 30 to 45 minutes. To use as main dish, add layer of chopped cooked chicken over tortilla strips.
Yield: 8 servings.

Approx Per Serving: *Cal 520; Prot 12.5 g; Carbo 35.9 g; T Fat 38.3 g; Chol 74.5 mg; Potas 309.0 mg; Sod 396.0 mg.*

Eloise B. Kline
Whittier, California

PICKLED BEETS

Beets
1/2 cup vinegar
1/4 cup water
1/4 cup sugar
1 clove of garlic, minced

Cook and peel beets. Cut beets as desired. Pack into hot sterlized 1-pint jar. Combine vinegar, water, sugar and garlic in saucepan. Bring to a boil. Pour over beets, leaving 1/2-inch head space; seal with 2-piece lids. Cool. Store in refrigerator.
Yield: 1 pint.

Nutritional information is not available.

Leslie Owens
Dallas, Texas

GRANDMA'S PICKLED EGGS

This easy, make-ahead recipe is at least 100 years old.

2   16-ounce cans sliced
     beets
2 cups cider vinegar
²/₃ cup sugar
6 whole cloves
2 cinnamon sticks
1 teaspoon ginger
1 teaspoon whole
     peppercorns
2 bay leaves
¹/₄ teaspoon caraway seed
12 hard-boiled eggs

Drain beets, reserving liquid. Place reserved liquid from canned beets in medium saucepan. Add vinegar, sugar, cloves, cinnamon sticks, ginger, peppercorns, bay leaves and caraway seed. Bring to a simmer. Simmer for 1 or 2 minutes, stirring frequently. Cool to room temperature. Alternate layers of sliced beets and eggs in sterilized ¹/₂-gallon jar. Pour liquid over beets and eggs. Chill, covered, in refrigerator for 48 hours or longer. For extra zip add 4 small yellow pickled peppers. Yield: 12 servings.

Approx Per Serving: *Cal 153; Prot 6.9 g; Carbo 20.0 g; T Fat 5.7 g; Chol 274.0 mg; Potas 226.0 mg; Sod 277.0 mg.*

Judy Reno
Riverside, California

TEMPURA BATTER FOR MEAT AND FISH

I got this recipe in a French cooking class. It is the best, lightest and most crisp coating that I have ever eaten.

2 cups plus 1 tablespoon
     flour
2 tablespoons plus
     1¹/₂ teaspoons melted
     butter
2 cups warm water

Combine flour and butter in bowl; mix well. Add water, stirring until smooth. Let stand, covered, in refrigerator 2 hours or longer. Soak meat or fish in milk; drain. Dip into batter to coat. Deep-fry in hot oil. Yield: 4 servings.

Approx Per Serving: *Cal 298; Prot 6.8 g; Carbo 49.0 g; T Fat 7.8 g; Chol 19.4 mg; Potas 63.7 mg; Sod 61.8 mg.*

Martha Haven
Grand Junction, Colorado

TERIYAKI MARINADE

1 cup Brandy
1 cup soy sauce
1 cup pineapple-apricot
  nectar
1 cup packed brown sugar.
2 tablespoons minced
  garlic
1 teaspoon ground ginger

Combine Brandy, soy sauce, nectar, brown sugar, garlic and ginger in saucepan. Simmer for 10 minutes, stirring frequently. Store in refrigerator. Use on pork, ribs, steak or chicken. Marinate meat for 1 hour before cooking. Yield: 4 cups.

Approx Per Cup: *Cal 429; Prot 4.7 g; Carbo 92.5 g; T Fat 0.2 g; Chol 0.0 mg; Potas 443.0 mg; Sod 4145.0 mg.*

Karen Spitzer
Temecula, California

A BEST FRIEND'S BARBECUE SAUCE

3/4 cup catsup
3/4 cup cold water
3 tablespoons liquid smoke
2 tablespoons vinegar
1 tablespoon
  Worcestershire sauce
3 tablespoons brown sugar
1 teaspoon salt
2 1/4 teaspoons chili powder

Combine catsup, water, liquid smoke, vinegar, Worcestershire sauce, brown sugar, salt and chili powder in saucepan. Bring to a boil over low heat, stirring frequently. Use on ribs or other meat. Store in refrigerator or freezer. For thicker sauce, omit water. Yield: 2 cups.

Approx Per Cup: *Cal 202; Prot 2.4 g; Carbo 49.5 g; T Fat 0.9 g; Chol 0.0 mg; Potas 572.0 mg; Sod 2244.0 mg.*

Marian Studer
Lexington, Kentucky

ORANGE SAUCE FOR DUCK À L'ORANGE

The Bourbon Barrel Hunt Club of Michigan has used this recipe for years and it is especially delicious and easy to make.

4 cups orange marmalade
1/4 cup butter
1 tablespoon seasoning
  salt
1 tablespoon onion salt
2 tablespoons basil
1 cup white wine

Combine marmalade, butter, seasoning salt, onion salt, basil and wine in saucepan. Simmer for 1 hour, stirring frequently. Strain while hot. May make ahead and reheat. Yield: 5 cups.

Approx Per Cup: *Cal 783; Prot 0.7 g; Carbo 179.0 g; T Fat 9.3 g; Chol 24.8 mg; Potas 1669.0 mg; Sod 2690.0 mg.*

Judith Forbis, Ansata Arabian Stud
Mena, Arkansas

Oats, Grains and Other Rations

Breads

JOHN WYATT'S CHEESE BISCUITS

This is a great biscuit to have with a drink.

1 cup butter, softened
8 ounces Romano cheese
1 cup flour
1 cup self-rising flour
1 tablespoon cornmeal
1/8 teaspoon salt
1/8 teaspoon cayenne
　pepper
1/8 teaspoon chili powder

Cream butter and cheese in bowl until light and fluffy. Add sifted mixture of flour, cornmeal, salt, cayenne and chili powder; mix well. Knead on floured surface. Roll as for biscuits. Cut with biscuit cutter. Place in 9x9-inch baking dish. Bake at 250 degrees for 40 to 45 minutes or until brown. Cool. Yield: 8 servings.

Approx Per Serving: *Cal 446; Prot 14.0 g; Carbo 25.5 g; T Fat 32.2 g; Chol 95.1 mg; Potas 72.8 mg; Sod 792.0 mg.*

John Wyatt
Queensland, Australia

MARGARET CRAWFORD'S SPOON BREAD

1 cup yellow cornmeal
1/3 cup water
1 cup hominy grits
3 cups water
1/4 teaspoon salt
1/4 cup butter
1 egg, slightly beaten
1/2 cup evaporated milk
1/2 cup water
1 teaspoon baking
　powder

Combine cornmeal and 1/3 cup water in bowl; mix well. Let stand for several minutes. Cook grits in 3 cups water with salt in saucepan over medium heat for 15 minutes or until thickened, stirring constantly. Stir in butter until melted. Cool. Add to cornmeal mixture; mix well. Add egg, evaporated milk mixed with 1/2 cup water, baking powder and salt to taste. Pour into greased 9x9-inch loaf pan. Place in larger pan of water. Bake at 350 degrees for 60 to 75 minutes or until brown. Reduce temperature if spoon bread browns too fast. Yield: 12 servings.

Approx Per Serving: *Cal 139; Prot 3.3 g; Carbo 18.9 g; T Fat 5.7 g; Chol 36.3 mg; Potas 85.1 mg; Sod 93.7 mg.*

Chaille Groom Trevor, Brusally Ranch
Scottsdale, Arizona

HOLIDAY DATE BREAD

1 cup chopped dates
1 teaspoon soda
1 cup boiling water
1 cup sugar
2 eggs, slightly beaten
2 tablespoons melted
  butter
1¹/₂ cups flour
1 teaspoon vanilla extract
1 cup chopped pecans

Combine dates, soda and boiling water in bowl. Let stand until cool. Combine sugar, eggs, butter, flour and vanilla in bowl; mix well. Add date mixture; mix well. Fold in pecans. Pour into greased 5x9-inch loaf pan. Bake at 325 degrees for 1 hour. Yield: 12 slices.

Approx Per Slice: *Cal 192; Prot 3.0 g; Carbo 39.5 g; T Fat 3.1 g; Chol 50.8 mg; Potas 124.0 mg; Sod 97.2 mg.*

Mary Jane Parkinson
El Cajon, California

SOUR CREAM GINGERBREAD

2 eggs
¹/₂ cup sour cream
¹/₂ cup molasses
³/₄ cup packed brown
  sugar
3 cups flour
1 teaspoon soda
1 teaspoon ginger
¹/₄ teaspoon salt
¹/₂ cup melted butter

Combine eggs, sour cream, molasses and brown sugar in mixer bowl; beat well. Add sifted mixture of flour, soda, ginger and salt; mix well. Stir in butter. Pour into greased 9x9-inch baking dish. Bake at 350 degrees for 30 minutes or until gingerbread tests done. Cut into squares. Melted butter is not essential, but it keeps the gingerbread moist and fresh for days, if it lasts that long. Yield: 12 servings.

Approx Per Serving: *Cal 296; Prot 4.7 g; Carbo 45.0 g; T Fat 10.9 g; Chol 70.6 mg; Potas 228.0 mg; Sod 203.0 mg.*

Belle Walters
Acton, California

POPOVERS

This is an old family recipe that works every time!

2 eggs
1 cup milk
1 tablespoon oil
1 cup sifted flour
1/4 teaspoon salt
22 tablespoons oil

Combine eggs, milk and 1 tablespoon oil in blender container; process until smooth. Sift in flour and salt. Process for 4 minutes. Place 1 tablespoon oil in each muffin cup. Heat in oven until oil is sizzling. Pour batter into muffin cups. Bake at 450 degrees for 15 minutes. Reduce temperature to 350 degrees. Bake for 15 minutes longer. Yield: 22 servings.

Approx Per Serving: *Cal 164; Prot 1.5 g; Carbo 4.6 g; T Fat 15.8 g; Chol 26.4 mg; Potas 26.0 mg; Sod 35.2 mg.*

Mrs. R.E. Newman
Morrison, Colorado

BREAD OF DON CERVAISÉ

2 tablespoons dry yeast
2 tablespoons sugar
2 1/2 cups warm water
7 cups bread flour
1 tablespoon salt
1 egg white, well beaten
2 tablespoons sesame
  seed

Dissolve yeast and sugar in 1/2 cup warm water in mixer bowl. Add remaining 2 cups warm water, flour and salt. Mix with dough hook for 15 minutes. Place in greased bowl, turning to coat surface. Let rise, covered, until doubled in bulk. Divide dough into 3 portions. Knead each portion briefly. Shape each into long loaf; place in French bread pans. Let rise, covered, until doubled in bulk. Brush with egg white; sprinkle with sesame seed. Slash each loaf diagonally 3 times. Bake at 450 degrees for 10 minutes. Reduce temperature to 350 degrees. Bake for 5 to 10 minutes longer. Remove loaves from pans immediately. Cover with cloth. Let stand until cool enough to eat. A warm humid kitchen or a pan of water placed in the bottom of the oven during baking will greatly improve the moistness of this bread. Yield: 24 servings.

Approx Per Serving: *Cal 139; Prot 4.2 g; Carbo 28.8 g; T Fat 0.4 g; Chol 0.0 mg; Potas 49.2 mg; Sod 270.0 mg.*

Don Severa
Templeton, California

HOME BAKED BREAD MADE EASY

*This recipe has been passed down in our family from the
times when bread was made daily.*

2 packages dry yeast
3/4 cup warm water
1 cup evaporated milk
1 cup boiling water
2 eggs, slightly beaten
1/4 cup sugar
2 teaspoons salt
5 tablespoons melted
   shortening
6 1/2 cups (about) flour

Dissolve yeast in 3/4 cup warm water. Scald milk in saucepan. Combine milk and 1 cup boiling water in large bowl. Cool to lukewarm. Add eggs, sugar, salt, shortening and yeast; mix well. Add 5 1/2 cups flour; beat until well mixed. Mix to form soft dough. Knead in enough remaining flour to make medium dough. Let rise, covered, for 1 hour. Divide dough into 2 portions. Shape into loaves. Place in greased 5x9-inch loaf pans. Let rise, covered, for 1 hour. Bake at 375 degrees for 20 minutes or until loaves test done. This recipe may be used for dinner rolls, cinnamon rolls, doughnuts or coffee cake. Add 6 tablespoons sugar when making sweet breads or doughnuts. Let dough rise twice. Yield: 24 slices.

Approx Per Slice: *Cal 177; Prot 5.0 g; Carbo 29.1 g; T Fat 4.3 g; Chol 25.9 mg;
Potas 81.2 mg; Sod 196.0 mg.*

*Barbara Carabeo
McNeal, Arizona*

NATURAL OAT BREAD

1/4 cup butter
1 2/3 cups evaporated milk
3/4 cup water
2 tablespoons honey
1 tablespoon salt
2 packages dry yeast
4 to 5 cups flour
1/2 cup wheat germ
1 1/3 cups oats

Melt butter in saucepan. Add evaporated milk, water, honey and salt; mix well. Heat to 110 degrees. Add yeast; stir until dissolved. Combine flour, wheat germ and oats in large bowl; mix well. Add yeast mixture; mix well. Knead on floured surface for 8 minutes or until smooth and elastic. Place in greased bowl, turning to coat surface. Let rise, covered, for 1 to 1 1/2 hours or until doubled in bulk. Divide dough into 2 portions. Shape into loaves. Place in greased 4x8-inch loaf pans. Let rise until doubled in bulk. Bake at 350 degrees for 35 minutes. Yield: 24 servings.

Approx Per Serving: *Cal 146; Prot 4.7 g; Carbo 23.0 g; T Fat 3.9 g; Chol 10.3 mg;
Potas 115.0 mg; Sod 302.0 mg.*

*Mary Jo and Bob Larum
Elbert, Colorado*

SOURDOUGH SCONES

This is not an easy recipe, but it is worth all the work. I found it while on a skiing trip in Sun Valley.

1 cup Sourdough Starter
2 cups flour
2 cups milk
Oil for deep frying

Combine Starter, flour and milk in bowl; mix well. Let stand at room temperature for 8 hours to overnight. Remove 1 cup mixture. Add to Starter; mix well. Knead remaining mixture on floured surface until smooth and elastic. Place in greased bowl, turning to coat surface. Let rise, covered, until doubled in bulk. Pinch quarter-sized pieces from dough. Roll into balls; press to flatten. Place on greased baking sheet. Let rise until doubled in bulk. Deep-fry scones until golden brown. Serve warm with butter and honey. Yield: 36 scones.

Nutritional information is not available.

Sourdough Starter

1 cup shredded raw
  potato
4 cups water
1 tablespoon salt
1 tablespoon sugar
1 tablespoon flour
1 package dry yeast

Combine potato, water, salt, sugar and flour in saucepan. Bring to a boil. Cook until clear, stirring constantly. Cool. Add yeast; mix well. Let stand, covered lightly, at room temperature for 24 hours or longer before using. Starter should be used at least once a week and stored in refrigerator when not in use. Starter may separate but is all right to use. Discard Starter if it turns orange.

Nutritional information is not available.

Diane Fortuna
Santa Barbara, California

Sweet Feed

Desserts

PLUM PUDDING

This is a traditional Christmas dish in Great Britain.

1 pound dried currants
2 cups chopped suet
1 pound raisins
1/2 cup chopped citron
1 cup flour, sifted
1 nutmeg, grated
1/2 teaspoon mace
1 tablespoon cinnamon
1 teaspoon salt
1/2 cup packed brown
  sugar
7 egg yolks
1/4 cup cream
1/2 cup Brandy
3 cups fine white bread
  crumbs
7 egg whites

Rinse currants. Combine suet, raisins, currants and citron in bowl. Add a small amount of flour; stir until suet and fruit are coated. Sift remaining flour with spices, salt and brown sugar into large bowl. Add suet mixture; mix well. Add egg yolks, cream, Brandy and bread crumbs; mix well. Beat egg whites until stiff peaks form. Fold stiffly beaten egg whites into crumb mixture gently. Pour into greased 4-quart mold. Place in steamer. Steam for 6 hours. Let stand for several minutes. Unmold onto serving plate. Serve with hot wine sauce. Yield: 24 servings.

Approx Per Serving: *Cal 211; Prot 4.9 g;) 41.2 g; T Fat 3.4 g; Chol 83.9 mg; Potas 256.0 mg; Sod 207.0 Nutritional information does not in. ıet.*

Mrs. Ian Hedley, Briery Close Stud
Windermere Cumbria, England

ARABIAN DATES WITH SESAME SEED (Tamr Bel Simsim)

9 ounces almonds
1/4 cup corn oil
1 cup sesame seed
2 1/4 pounds pitted soft
  dates, chopped
1 tablespoon cardamom

Blanch almonds. Remove skins and split into halves. Fry in oil until golden brown. Drain on paper towel. Sprinkle sesame seed in ungreased skillet. Heat until golden, stirring constantly. Spread on tray. Combine dates and cardamom in bowl, mixing until dough-like. Pinch off date-sized pieces. Shape into fingers around almond halves. Roll in sesame seed, coating well. Yield: 10 servings.

Nutritional information is not available.

*Excerpted from **Aramco World***

RICH APRICOT PASTRY

1 cup butter, softened
2 cups flour
1 cup sour cream
1 cup apricot jam
1 cup chopped walnuts
1/2 cup sifted
   confectioners' sugar

Mix butter and flour in mixer bowl until crumbly. Add sour cream; mix well. Shape into ball; wrap in waxed paper. Chill overnight. Divide into 4 portions. Roll each into 12-inch square on floured surface. Spread with jam and walnuts. Roll as for jelly roll. Place seam side down in greased 12x16-inch baking pan. Bake at 350 degrees for 30 to 35 minutes or until golden brown. Cool. Sprinkle with confectioners' sugar. Cut each pastry into 8 pieces. May add raisins, coconut, chocolate chips or chocolate filling if desired. Yield: 32 servings.

Approx Per Serving: *Cal 152; Prot 1.7 g; Carbo 15.5 g; T Fat 9.7 g; Chol 18.7 mg; Potas 47.5 mg; Sod 53.8 mg.*

Diane Fortuna
Santa Barbara, California

CHEESECAKE

1 1/2 cups graham cracker
   crumbs
1/3 cup melted butter
4 eggs
1 cup sugar
16 ounces cream cheese,
   softened
1 teaspoon vanilla extract
2 cups sour cream
10 tablespoons sugar
2 teaspoons vanilla
   extract

Mix cracker crumbs and butter in bowl. Press into 9x13-inch baking pan. Bake at 375 degrees for 5 to 8 minutes or until light brown. Reduce temperature to 325 degrees. Beat eggs in bowl until thick and lemon-colored. Cream 1 cup sugar, cream cheese and 1 teaspoon vanilla in mixer bowl until light and fluffy. Beat in eggs. Spoon into prepared pan. Bake at 325 degrees for 30 minutes or until set. Mix sour cream, 10 tablespoons sugar and 2 teaspoons vanilla in bowl. Spread on cheesecake. Bake for 10 minutes longer. Cool completely on wire rack. Store in refrigerator. Yield: 24 servings.

Approx Per Serving: *Cal 227; Prot 3.6 g; Carbo 20.7 g; T Fat 14.8 g; Chol 81.6 mg; Potas 81.6 mg; Sod 145.0 mg.*

Betty Zekan
Richfield, Ohio

CHOCOLATE CHEESECAKE

*Place a large spoon on cookie crust and pour filling into spoon
to keep crumbs from mixing with filling.*

16 ounces chocolate
    sandwich cookies
24 ounces cream cheese,
    softened
1 cup sugar
2 teaspoons vanilla
    extract
3 eggs
1 cup sour cream
3 tablespoons baking
    cocoa

Process cookies into crumbs in food processor container. Press over bottom and 2 inches up side of 9-inch springform pan. Process cream cheese in food processor container until fluffy. Add sugar and vanilla gradually. Blend in eggs 1 at a time. Add sour cream and cocoa; process until smooth. Spoon into prepared pan. Bake at 350 degrees for 1 hour or until set. Turn off oven; leave oven door ajar. Let stand in oven for 1 hour. Yield: 12 servings.

Approx Per Serving: *Cal 491; Prot 6.9 g; Carbo 47.0 g; T Fat 31.6 g; Chol 70.4 mg;
Potas 174.0 mg; Sod 357.0 mg.*

*Don Miller
Shreveport, Louisiana*

CHEESECAKE WITH STRAWBERRY SAUCE

This is my original recipe. The lemon gives it a distinctive flavor.

1/4 cup sugar
1/4 cup butter, softened
1 1/2 cups graham cracker
    crumbs
32 ounces cream cheese,
    softened
3/4 cup sugar
3 eggs
1/4 cup lemon juice
Grated rind of 1 lemon
1 teaspoon lemon extract
3/4 cup sour cream
1 tablespoon
    confectioners' sugar
1 10-ounce package
    frozen sweetened
    strawberries
2 tablespoons sugar
2 tablespoons cornstarch
1 teaspoon lemon juice

Mix 1/4 cup sugar and butter in bowl. Reserve 2 tablespoons crumbs. Add remaining crumbs to butter mixture; mix well. Press over bottom and side of springform pan. Bake at 395 degrees for 8 minutes. Cool. Beat cream cheese with 3/4 cup sugar, eggs, 1/4 cup lemon juice, lemon rind and lemon extract in mixer bowl until smooth. Spoon into prepared pan. Bake at 300 degrees for 25 minutes. Spread with mixture of sour cream and confectioners' sugar. Bake for 10 minutes. Top with reserved crumbs. Cool on wire rack. Drain strawberries, reserving juice. Blend reserved juice with 2 tablespoons sugar and cornstarch in saucepan. Cook until thickened, stirring constantly. Stir in 1 teaspoon lemon juice and food coloring if desired. Cool. Stir in strawberries. Chill until serving time. Yield: 10 servings.

Approx Per Serving: *Cal 621; Prot 10.7 g; Carbo 50.2 g; T Fat 43.4 g; Chol 201.0 mg;
Potas 244.0 mg; Sod 450.0 mg.*

*Marie Jo Anderson
Austin, Texas*

DOROTHE'S FAMOUS CHEESECAKE

11 ounces cream cheese
3/4 cup sugar
2 eggs
2 tablespoons lemon juice
3/4 teaspoon vanilla extract
1 graham cracker pie shell
3 tablespoons sugar
8 ounces sour cream

Soften cream cheese. Combine with 3/4 cup sugar and eggs in mixer bowl; beat until smooth. Add lemon juice and vanilla. Pour into pie shell. Bake at 350 degrees for 20 minutes. Blend 3 tablespoons sugar with sour cream. Spread over top. Bake for 10 minutes. Cool. Chill for 6 hours or longer. Yield: 8 servings.

Approx Per Serving: *Cal 512; Prot 7.1 g; Carbo 51.6 g; T Fat 31.8 g; Chol 124.0 mg; Potas 171.0 mg; Sod 388.0 mg.*

Dorothe Fisher
Billings, Montana

LOIS'S CHOCOLATE DESSERT

1 stack butter crackers
1/2 cup melted butter
1   4-ounce package chocolate instant pudding mix
1 cup milk
2 cups ice cream, softened
8 ounces whipped topping

Crush butter crackers. Mix cracker crumbs and butter in bowl. Press over bottom of 9x13-inch dish. Combine pudding mix, milk and ice cream in bowl; mix well. Spoon into prepared dish. Let stand for several minutes. Top with whipped topping. Yield: 12 servings.

Approx Per Serving: *Cal 236; Prot 2.8 g; Carbo 23.9 g; T Fat 15.7 g; Chol 35.2 mg; Potas 112.0 mg; Sod 248.0 mg.*

Audrey Hopkins
Fremont, Michigan

ÉCLAIR CAKE

8 ounces cream cheese
1 cup margarine
1 cup water
1 cup flour
4 eggs
2   4-ounce packages vanilla instant pudding mix
4 cups milk
8 ounces whipped topping
1/3 cup hot fudge topping

Soften cream cheese. Bring margarine and water to a boil in saucepan, stirring until margarine is melted; remove from heat. Stir in flour. Cool for 5 minutes. Stir in eggs 1 at a time. Spread in 9x13-inch baking dish. Bake at 400 degrees for 30 minutes; do not overbake. Cool. Prepare pudding mix with milk according to package directions. Add cream cheese; beat until smooth. Spoon over cooled layer. Top with whipped topping. Drizzle with fudge topping. Chill. Yield: 15 servings.

Approx Per Serving: *Cal 360; Prot 6.8 g; Carbo 30.2 g; T Fat 24.0 g; Chol 99.9 mg; Potas 175.0 mg; Sod 352.0 mg.*

Joanne Martin
Ontario, New York

FLAN WITH ALMONDS

This caramel custard is an excellent light dessert to serve after a heavy meal.

1/2 cup almonds
1/2 cup sugar
5 eggs
1/2 cup sugar
1/4 teaspoon salt
1 teaspoon vanilla extract
31/2 cups milk
1 cup strawberries
1 cup drained pineapple
    chunks
8 ounces seedless green
    grapes

Place almonds on baking sheet. Toast in 325-degree oven for 6 to 7 minutes or just until golden brown. Sprinkle evenly in 5-cup ring mold. Place mold in shallow baking pan. Sprinkle 1/2 cup sugar evenly in small heavy skillet. Cook over very low heat until sugar melts to a golden syrup, stirring occasionally with wooden spoon. Pour into ring mold, tilting to coat bottom and side. Cool; syrup will harden. Beat eggs, 1/2 cup sugar, salt and vanilla in large bowl with wire whisk. Add milk gradually, beating until smooth but not frothy. Reserve 1 cup mixture. Pour remaining egg mixture into prepared mold. Place on middle rack of oven. Add reserved egg mixture. Pour hot water 1 inch deep in pan. Bake at 325 degrees for 55 to 60 minutes or until knife inserted 1 inch from edge comes out clean; do not overbake. Remove mold to wire rack to cool. Chill for 1 to 24 hours. Loosen side with spatula. Invert onto serving plate. Toss fruit lightly in bowl. Spoon into center of mold. Spoon caramel sauce over servings of custard and fruit. Yield: 8 servings.

Approx Per Serving: *Cal 303; Prot 9.4 g; Carbo 42.5 g; T Fat 11.7 g; Chol 186.0 mg; Potas 363.0 mg; Sod 157.0 mg.*

Jennifer Jo Bird, Jen-Mar Arabians
Manor, Texas

THE BEST FROZEN DESSERT EVER

This is my mother's all-time favorite. It is served at nearly
every card party and family gathering.

24 vanilla sandwich
    cookies, crushed
28 ounces whipped
    topping
1/2 gallon pecan praline
    ice cream
1 cup chopped pecans

Mix cookie crumbs and whipped topping in bowl. Spread half the mixture in 9x13-inch dish. Top with ice cream and remaining cookie mixture. Sprinkle with pecans. Freeze until firm. May substitute your choice of cookies, ice cream flavor and nuts. Yield: 24 servings.

Approx Per Serving: *Cal 234; Prot 3.7 g; Carbo 24.2 g; T Fat 14.2 g; Chol 23.0 mg; Potas 172.0 mg; Sod 108.0 mg.*

Loren Collins, Triangle LP Arabians
Fort Collins, Colorado

MARIE'S FRUIT COBBLER

This favorite recipe was given to me by Louise Seydler many years ago. Do not use low calorie margarine or milk with less than 2% butterfat in it.

5 cups sliced peaches
1/4 cup sugar
Juice of 1 lemon
1/4 cup butter
1 cup flour
1 cup sugar
2 teaspoons baking
  powder
1/2 teaspoon salt
1 cup milk

Mix peaches, 1/4 cup sugar and lemon juice in bowl. Melt butter in 8x8-inch glass baking dish. Spoon fruit into dish. Combine flour, 1 cup sugar, baking powder, salt and milk in bowl; mix well. Batter will be thin. Pour evenly over fruit. Bake at 375 degrees for 35 to 40 minutes or until cobbler is bubbly and top is brown. May substitute berries or other fruit for peaches if preferred. Yield: 6 servings.

Approx Per Serving: *Cal 396; Prot 4.7 g; Carbo 77.1 g; T Fat 9.4 g; Chol 26.2 mg; Potas 384.0 mg; Sod 371.0 mg.*

Marie Jo Anderson
Austin, Texas

LEMON PRETZEL TORTE

1/2 cup butter, softened
1/2 cup sugar
1 1/2 cups coarsely
  crushed pretzels
1   3-ounce package
  lemon pudding and pie
  filling mix
2   3-ounce packages
  whipped topping mix
1 cup confectioners' sugar
8 ounces cream cheese,
  softened

Cream butter and sugar in mixer bowl until light and fluffy. Add pretzels; mix with hands. Press over bottom of 9x13-inch dish. Chill in refrigerator. Cook pudding and pie filling mix according to package directions. Cool. Prepare whipped topping mix according to package directions. Cream confectioners' sugar and cream cheese in mixer bowl until light. Add whipped topping; mix well. Spread over chilled crust. Top with cooled pudding. Chill overnight. Yield: 12 servings.

Approx Per Serving: *Cal 345; Prot 4.7 g; Carbo 48.7 g; T Fat 17.1 g; Chol 42.8 mg; Potas 75.9 mg; Sod 631.0 mg.*

Jill S. Myles
Fort Collins, Colorado

LEMON PUDDING

1 cup sugar
1 tablespoon butter
2 tablespoons flour
Juice of 1½ lemons
Grated rind of 1½
  lemons
1 cup milk
3 egg yolks
3 egg whites

Combine sugar, butter, flour, lemon juice, lemon rind, milk and egg yolks in bowl in order listed; mix until smooth. Beat egg whites in mixer bowl until stiff peaks form. Fold into lemon mixture. Spoon into 4 greased individual pudding molds. Set molds in shallow pan of water. Bake at 300 degrees just until knife inserted in center comes out clean; do not overbake. Yield: 4 servings.

Approx Per Serving: *Cal 345; Prot 7.3 g; Carbo 61.8 g; T Fat 9.3 g; Chol 222.0 mg; Potas 218.0 mg; Sod 103.0 mg.*

Leslie Owens
Dallas, Texas

PEACH COBBLER

This can be served warm or cold. It reheats well in the microwave for a fresh-baked taste.

2 cups flour
¼ teaspoon baking
  powder
3 tablespoons sugar
½ teaspoon salt
½ cup butter
4 cups frozen
  unsweetened peach
  slices
¾ cup (about) sugar
1½ teaspoons cinnamon
2 egg yolks
1 cup cream

Combine flour, baking powder, 3 tablespoons sugar, salt and butter in food processor container; process until mixed. Press over bottom and sides of 7x11-inch glass baking dish. Place peaches in prepared dish. Sprinkle with ¾ cup sugar and cinnamon. Bake at 400 degrees for 15 minutes. Beat egg yolks and cream in mixer bowl until smooth. Pour over peaches. Bake for 30 minutes longer. Yield: 10 servings.

Approx Per Serving: *Cal 434; Prot 4.4 g; Carbo 62.7 g; T Fat 19.5 g; Chol 112.0 mg; Potas 180.0 mg; Sod 210.0 mg.*

Don Miller
Shreveport, Louisiana

PEARS IN RED WINE

This is a wonderful light dessert after a heavy meal. Be sure to use good quality pears and wine.

10 tablespoons sugar
3/4 cup red wine
3/4 cup water
1 strip lemon rind
1 1-inch cinnamon stick
6 firm ripe pears
1 teaspoon arrowroot
1 tablespoon water
1/4 cup toasted slivered
  almonds

Combine sugar, wine and 3/4 cup water in saucepan. Heat until sugar is dissolved. Add lemon rind and cinnamon. Bring to a boil. Cook for 1 minute. Peel pears, leaving stems intact. Place in small deep saucepan. Add syrup, covering pears if possible. Simmer, covered, for 20 to 30 minutes or until tender, spooning syrup over any uncovered portions of pears. Remove and drain pears; place in serving bowl. Cook syrup until reduced to 1 1/4 cups; strain. Blend syrup with mixture of arrowroot and 1 tablespoon water in saucepan. Cook until thickened, stirring constantly. Spoon over pears. Chill until serving time. Sprinkle with almonds. Yield: 6 servings.

Approx Per Serving: *Cal 235; Prot 1.9 g; Carbo 48.2 g; T Fat 3.6 g; Chol 0.0 mg; Potas 290.0 mg; Sod 3.7 mg.*

Jennifer Jo Bird, Jen-Mar Arabians
Manor, Texas

RASPBERRY TRIFLE

I am always asked to bring this to church socials and family reunions.

2 4-ounce packages
  vanilla instant
  pudding mix
6 cups milk
24 ladyfingers, split
2 10-ounce packages
  frozen raspberries,
  thawed
1/2 cup Sherry
16 ounces whipped
  topping

Prepare pudding mix with milk according to package directions. Layer ladyfingers, raspberries, Sherry, pudding and whipped topping 1/3 at a time in large glass bowl. Chill until serving time. May substitute thinly sliced pound cake for ladyfingers if preferred. Yield: 12 servings.

Approx Per Serving: *Cal 374; Prot 6.7 g; Carbo 56.7 g; T Fat 13.0 g; Chol 20.3 mg; Potas 316.0 mg; Sod 298.0 mg.*

Deirdre Janney, Ph.D.
Lucedale, Mississippi

STRAWBERRY DESSERT

I have served this easy dessert at dinner parties for 35 or 40 years.

3 egg whites
1 cup sugar
1 teaspoon vanilla extract
24 soda crackers, crushed
1/4 teaspoon baking
powder
1/2 cup chopped pecans
3 10-ounce packages
frozen sliced
strawberries
1 cup whipping cream
1 tablespoon sugar

Beat egg whites in mixer bowl until soft peaks form. Add 1 cup sugar and vanilla, beating until stiff peaks form. Mix cracker crumbs and baking powder in bowl. Fold in egg whites and pecans. Spoon into buttered 9x12-inch baking dish. Bake at 350 degrees for 30 minutes. Cool completely. Spread with strawberries. Whip cream in mixer bowl until soft peaks form. Mix in 1 tablespoon sugar. Spread over strawberries. Chill for 24 hours or longer. Cut into squares. Yield: 9 servings.

Approx Per Serving: *Cal 378; Prot 2.8 g; Carbo 60.8 g; T Fat 15.1 g; Chol 38.9 mg; Potas 213.0 mg; Sod 142.0 mg.*

Anita R. Kamperman
Dallas, Texas

APPLESAUCE CAKE

2 cups flour
1 teaspoon soda
1 teaspoon cinnamon
1 teaspoon cloves
1/4 cup butter, softened
1/4 cup lard, softened
1 1/2 cups packed brown
sugar
1 egg
1 1/2 cups sweetened
applesauce
1 cup raisins
1/2 cup chopped walnuts

Sift flour, soda, cinnamon and cloves together 4 times. Cream butter, lard and brown sugar in bowl until light and fluffy. Add egg and applesauce; mix well. Add flour mixture, raisins and walnuts; mix well. Pour into greased 9x13-inch baking pan. Bake at 350 degrees for 40 minutes. Cut into squares. Yield: 12 servings.

Approx Per Serving: *Cal 356; Prot 4.0 g; Carbo 60.9 g; T Fat 12.0 g; Chol 37.2 mg; Potas 272.0 mg; Sod 123.0 mg.*

Syl Crooker
Mankato, Minnesota

CARROT CAKE

4 eggs, slightly beaten
2 cups sugar
1½ cups oil
2 cups flour
2 teaspoons cinnamon
1 teaspoon soda
1 teaspoon baking
  powder
1 teaspoon salt
4 cups shredded carrots
¾ cup chopped walnuts
1 cup butter, softened
1 16-ounce package
  confectioners' sugar
8 ounces cream cheese,
  softened

Cream eggs and sugar in mixer bowl until light and fluffy. Add oil gradually, beating until smooth. Sift in flour, cinnamon, soda, baking powder and salt; mix well. Fold in carrots and nuts. Pour into 2 greased and floured 9-inch cake pans. Bake for 35 to 40 minutes or until cake tests done. Cool on wire rack. Cream butter, confectioners' sugar and cream cheese in bowl until light and fluffy. Spread between layers and over top and side of cake. Yield: 16 servings.

Approx Per Serving: *Cal 504; Prot 4.4 g; Carbo 41.0 g; T Fat 37.0 g; Chol 99.6 mg; Potas 155.0 mg; Sod 330.0 mg.*

Darlene Scudder
San Luis Obispo, California

CHOCOLATE CHIP CAKE

This is a quick, easy cake. It is sturdy enough for lunch boxes and potluck dinners. It is delicious, so I have heard; it always disappears so fast I may never know!

1¾ cups boiling water
½ cup butter
1 cup oats
1 cup packed brown
  sugar
1 cup sugar
2 eggs
1¾ cups flour
1 teaspoon soda
½ teaspoon salt
2 cups semisweet
  chocolate chips
1 tablespoon cocoa
¾ cup chopped walnuts

Combine water, butter and oats in bowl; stir until butter melts. Cool for 10 minutes. Add sugars and eggs; mix well. Add mixture of flour, soda and salt; mix well. Stir in 1 cup chocolate chips and cocoa; mix well. Pour into greased 9x13-inch baking dish. Sprinkle with walnuts and remaining chocolate chips. Bake at 350 degrees for 40 minutes. Yield: 12 servings.

Approx Per Serving: *Cal 498; Prot 6.4 g; Carbo 70.5 g; T Fat 24.1 g; Chol 66.4 mg; Potas 260.0 mg; Sod 247.0 mg.*

Bob and Judy Harvey
Lake Geneva, Wisconsin

KAHLUA CAKE

1 2-layer package chocolate-fudge cake mix
2 eggs
1/4 cup oil
1/2 cup Kahlua
2 cups sour cream
2 cups chocolate chips

Combine cake mix, eggs, oil, Kahlua and sour cream in bowl; mix well. Add chocolate chips; mix well. Pour into greased bundt pan. Bake at 350 degrees for 45 to 55 minutes or until cake tests done. Yield: 16 servings.

Approx Per Serving: *Cal 372; Prot 4.1 g; Carbo 41.9 g; T Fat 21.6 g; Chol 47.0 mg; Potas 126.0 mg; Sod 231.0 mg.*

Shirley Lerum
Bieber, California

KLAMT KIDS FAVORITE CHOCOLATE CAKE

A friend made this while we were on a fishing trip in Montana when we all got a "sweet tooth" and didn't have much on hand. It's quick, easy and good.

1/3 cup margarine
3 tablespoons (rounded) baking cocoa
1 cup flour
1 cup (scant) sugar
1 egg
1 teaspoon vanilla extract
1 cup milk
2 tablespoons vinegar
1 teaspoon soda

Melt margarine in saucepan. Add cocoa; mix well. Cool. Sift flour and sugar into bowl. Add egg, vanilla and cocoa mixture; mix well. Combine milk and vinegar in small bowl. Add soda; mix well. Stir into batter; mix well. Pour into greased and floured 8x8-inch baking pan. Bake at 350 degrees for 30 minutes. Yield: 8 servings.

Approx Per Serving: *Cal 255; Prot 3.8 g; Carbo 39.5 g; T Fat 9.8 g; Chol 38.4 mg; Potas 95.9 mg; Sod 214.0 mg.*

Dottie Weaver, Shifting Sands Ranch
Bicknell, Utah

CHOCOLATE SURPRISE CAKE

Ed has a lifelong dislike for sauerkraut, but not even he could identify it as the secret ingredient in this cake.

1 8-ounce can sauerkraut
1/2 cup butter, softened
11/2 cups sugar
3 eggs
1 teaspoon vanilla extract
2 cups sifted flour
1 teaspoon baking
  powder
1 teaspoon soda
1/4 teaspoon salt
1/2 cup baking cocoa
1 cup water
1 cup milk chocolate
  chips
1/4 cup butter
1/2 cup sour cream
1 teaspoon vanilla extract
1/4 teaspoon salt
23/4 cups sifted
  confectioners' sugar

Rinse, drain and finely chop sauerkraut. Cream 1/2 cup butter and sugar in mixer bowl until light and fluffy. Add eggs 1 at a time, beating well after each addition. Stir in 1 teaspoon vanilla. Sift flour, baking powder, soda, 1/4 teaspoon salt and cocoa together . Add to creamed mixture alternately with water, mixing well after each addition. Stir in sauerkraut. Pour into greased and floured 9x13-inch baking pan. Bake at 350 degrees for 35 to 40 minutes or until cake tests done. Cool. Melt chocolate chips and butter in saucepan. Cool slightly. Add sour cream, vanilla and salt; mix well. Stir in confectioners' sugar; mix well. Spread over cake. Cut into squares. Yield: 12 servings.

Approx Per Serving: *Cal 393; Prot 5.3 g; Carbo 50.7 g; T Fat 20.9 g; Chol 104.0 mg; Potas 176.0 mg; Sod 433.0 mg.*

Edwin A. and Shirley Bogucki
Racine, Wisconsin

KRAUT FUDGE SURPRISE CAKE

1/2 cup sauerkraut
11/2 cups sugar
2/3 cup shortening
1 teaspoon vanilla extract
1/4 teaspoon salt
1/2 cup baking cocoa
3 eggs
21/4 cups sifted flour
1 teaspoon baking
  powder
1 teaspoon soda
1 cup water

Rinse, drain and chop sauerkraut. Cream sugar and shortening in mixer bowl until light and fluffy. Add vanilla, salt and cocoa; beat at low speed for 5 minutes. Add eggs; beat well. Sift in flour, baking powder and soda; beat at medium speed. Add water; mix well. Fold in sauerkraut. Pour into greased and floured 9x13-inch baking pan. Bake at 375 degrees for 45 minutes. Frost with favorite frosting. Yield: 12 servings.

Approx Per Serving: *Cal 306; Prot 4.5 g; Carbo 43.7 g; T Fat 13.6 g; Chol 68.5 mg; Potas 96.4 mg; Sod 224.0 mg.*

Bazy Tankersley
Tucson, Arizona

ZUCCHINI CHOCOLATE CAKE

1/2 cup margarine,
  softened
1/2 cup oil
1 3/4 cups sugar
2 eggs
1/2 cup sour cream
1 teaspoon vanilla extract
2 1/2 cups flour
1/2 teaspoon salt
1 teaspoon soda
1/4 cup baking cocoa
2 cups shredded zucchini
2/3 cup semisweet
  chocolate chips

Cream margarine, oil, sugar and eggs in bowl until light and fluffy. Add sour cream and vanilla; mix well. Sift in flour, salt, soda and cocoa; mix well. Add zucchini; mix well. Pour into greased 9x13-inch baking pan. Sprinkle chocolate chips over batter. Bake at 325 degrees for 45 to 50 minutes or until cake tests done. This cake stays moist and needs no frosting. Yield: 12 servings.

Approx Per Serving: *Cal 444; Prot 5.1 g; Carbo 56.3 g; T Fat 23.6 g; Chol 49.9 mg; Potas 162.0 mg; Sod 266.0 mg.*

Ruth Mawby
Augusta, Michigan

TEXAS SHEET CAKE

This is a very rich cake. A little goes a long way. It's great for a potluck, a crowd or a horse show.

2 cups flour
1 teaspoon soda
2 cups sugar
3 tablespoons baking
  cocoa
3/4 cup butter, softened
1 cup water
1/2 cup buttermilk
2 eggs
1 teaspoon vanilla extract
1 cup chopped pecans
1/2 cup butter, softened
3 tablespoons baking
  cocoa
6 tablespoons water
1 teaspoon vanilla extract
1 16-ounce package
  confectioners' sugar

Combine flour, soda and sugar in bowl; mix well. Mix 3 tablespoons cocoa, 3/4 cup butter and water in saucepan. Bring to a boil. Pour over flour mixture; mix well. Cool slightly. Add buttermilk, eggs, 1 teaspoon vanilla and pecans; mix well. Pour into greased 10x15-inch baking pan. Bake at 350 degrees for 15 to 18 minutes or until cake tests done. Combine 1/2 cup butter, 3 tablespoons cocoa, 6 tablespoons water and 1 teaspoon vanilla in saucepan. Bring to a boil. Pour over confectioners' sugar in bowl; mix until smooth. Spread over warm cake. Yield: 16 servings.

Approx Per Serving: *Cal 348; Prot 3.7 g; Carbo 39.5 g; T Fat 20.7 g; Chol 73.4 mg; Potas 92.6 mg; Sod 190.0 mg.*

Leslie Donaldson
Cave Creek, Arizona

ORANGE-DATE CAKE

One time when my family visited Jimmy and Thelma Dean in Kentucky, Thelma brought one of these cakes out of the freezer and we tasted it for the first time. What a treat! It is great.

1½ cups chopped dates
1 cup chopped pecans
4 cups flour
1 cup shortening
2 cups sugar
4 eggs, separated
1⅓ cups buttermilk
1 teaspoon soda
2 teaspoons grated
  orange rind
1 cup orange juice
2 cups sugar
1 teaspoon grated orange
  rind

Coat dates and pecans with a small amount of flour. Sift flour 3 times. Cream shortening and 2 cups sugar in bowl until light and fluffy. Beat egg yolks. Add to shortening mixture; mix well. Stir in flour, dates, pecans, mixture of buttermilk and soda and 2 teaspoons orange rind; mix well. Beat egg whites in mixer bowl until stiff peaks form. Fold into cake batter gently. Pour into greased and waxed paper-lined tube pan. Bake at 300 degrees for 1½ hours. Combine orange juice, 2 cups sugar and 1 teaspoon orange rind in saucepan. Heat until sugar is dissolved. Cool. Pierce cake with toothpick. Reserve a small amount of orange juice mixture. Pour remaining orange juice mixture over cake. Invert cake onto serving plate. Drizzle with reserved juice mixture. Yield: 10 servings.

Approx Per Serving: *Cal 880; Prot 10.4 g; Carbo 144.0 g; T Fat 31.7 g; Chol 111.0 mg; Potas 397.0 mg; Sod 148.0 mg.*

Jennifer Jo Bird, Jen-Mar Arabians
Manor, Texas

EASY AND GOOD PINEAPPLE CAKE

1 2-layer package white
   cake mix
1 8-ounce can crushed
   pineapple
1 4-ounce package
   lemon instant
   pudding mix

Prepare and bake cake mix according to package directions using two 9-inch round cake pans. Combine pineapple and pudding mix in bowl; mix well. Spread between cake layers. Spread favorite frosting over top and side of cake. Yield: 12 servings.

Approx Per Serving: *Cal 232; Prot 1.9 g; Carbo 48.5 g; T Fat 3.6 g; Chol 0.0 mg; Potas 20.1 mg; Sod 325.0 mg.*

Louise H. Donoghue
Goliad, Texas

BROWN SUGAR POUND CAKE

3/4 cup unsalted butter
3/4 cup shortening
2¼ cups packed brown
  sugar
5 egg yolks, well beaten
3 cups flour
½ teaspoon baking
  powder
⅛ teaspoon salt
1 cup milk
1 cup chopped pecans
1 teaspoon vanilla extract
5 egg whites, stiffly
  beaten

Cream butter, shortening and brown sugar in bowl until light and fluffy. Add egg yolks; mix well. Sift flour, baking powder and salt together. Add to creamed mixture alternately with milk, ending with flour and mixing well after each addition. Add pecans and vanilla; mix well. Fold in egg whites gently. Fill greased and floured tube pan 3/4 full. Bake at 325 degrees for 1½ hours. Yield: 12 servings.

Approx Per Serving: *Cal 594; Prot 7.4 g; Carbo 66.6 g; T Fat 34.3 g; Chol 148.0 mg; Potas 269.0 mg; Sod 94.5 mg.*

Phil Witter, Live Oak Arabians
Baton Rouge, Louisiana

RHUBARB CAKE

½ cup margarine,
  softened
1½ cups packed brown
  sugar
1 egg
1 teaspoon vanilla extract
1 cup milk
2 cups flour
1 teaspoon soda
⅛ teaspoon salt
2 cups finely chopped
  rhubarb
1 cup coconut
½ cup packed brown
  sugar
½ teaspoon cinnamon

Cream margarine and 1½ cups brown sugar in bowl until light and fluffy. Add egg, vanilla and milk; mix well. Add mixture of flour, soda and salt; mix well. Fold in rhubarb. Pour into greased 9x13-inch baking pan. Mix coconut, ½ cup brown sugar and cinnamon in small bowl. Sprinkle over batter. Bake at 350 degrees for 40 to 45 minutes or until cake tests done. Yield: 12 servings.

Approx Per Serving: *Cal 333; Prot 3.8 g; Carbo 56.2 g; T Fat 11.0 g; Chol 25.6 mg; Potas 261.0 mg; Sod 228.0 mg.*

Debora S. Wilson
Parker, Colorado

SWEDISH PEPPARKAKA

I got this recipe from a fellow Swedish Gymnastic Club member in Brooklyn, New York many years ago. It's now a family favorite.

3 eggs
3 cups packed light
  brown sugar
5 tablespoons melted
  butter
1¹/2 teaspoons cloves
1¹/2 teaspoons cinnamon
2¹/2 cups flour
1 teaspoon baking
  powder
1¹/2 cups buttermilk
1 teaspoon soda

Combine eggs and sugar in bowl; mix well. Add butter, cloves and cinnamon; mix well. Add mixture of flour and baking powder alternately with mixture of milk and soda, mixing well after each addition. Pour into greased tube pan. Bake at 350 degrees for 1 hour. Cool on wire rack. Yield: 12 servings.

Approx Per Serving: *Cal 376; Prot 5.3 g; Carbo 74.9 g; T Fat 6.8 g; Chol 82.6 mg; Potas 283.0 mg; Sod 211.0 mg.*

Vivian Blomquist
Sylmar, California

STRAWBERRY TUNNEL CREAM CAKE

This cake is best when used at one time. It always attracts much comment and is a very pretty cake visually.

1 10-inch angel food
  cake
8 ounces cream cheese,
  softened
1 14-ounce can
  sweetened condensed
  milk
¹/4 cup lemon juice
1 teaspoon almond
  extract
2 cups sliced fresh
  strawberries
3 cups whipped topping

Cut 1 inch off top of cake. Scoop out center of cake leaving 1-inch wide walls and bottom. Reserve cake pieces. Beat cream cheese in mixer bowl until light and fluffy. Add milk; mix well. Stir in lemon juice and almond extract. Fold in cake pieces and strawberries. Spoon into cake cavity. Replace top. Chill in refrigerator for 3 hours. Frost cake with whipped topping. Garnish with strawberry halves. Chill in refrigerator until serving time. Yield: 12 servings.

Approx Per Serving: *Cal 343; Prot 8.1 g; Carbo 52.3 g; T Fat 12.2 g; Chol 33.9 mg; Potas 293.0 mg; Sod 382.0 mg.*

Liz Eberts
Temecula Valley Arabian Horse Association
Temecula, California

SUNSET CAKE

This is a very pretty and flavorful cake. It can be dressed up elegantly or served to children on napkins.

1 2-layer package yellow cake mix
1 3-ounce package butterscotch instant pudding mix
3 eggs
1 cup oil
1 cup water
1/4 cup melted margarine
1/4 cup orange juice
1 1/2 cups confectioners' sugar

Combine cake mix, pudding mix, eggs, oil and water in mixer bowl; beat at low speed until well blended. Beat at medium speed for 4 minutes. Pour into greased 9x13-inch pan. Bake at 350 degrees for 30 minutes or until cake tests done. Pierce hot cake with toothpick. Blend margarine, orange juice and enough confectioners' sugar to make thin glaze in small bowl. Drizzle orange glaze over cake. Yield: 12 servings.

Approx Per Serving: *Cal 474; Prot 3.4 g; Carbo 55.5 g; T Fat 26.9 g; Chol 68.5 mg; Potas 29.8 mg; Sod 372.0 mg.*

Joan Reno
Bucyrus, Kansas

VANILLA WAFER CAKE

I collect recipes and I have never seen this very moist and delicious cake in any other cookbook.

3/4 cup butter, softened
1 1/2 cups sugar
6 eggs
1 12-ounce package coarsely crushed vanilla wafers
1/2 cup milk
1 cup chopped walnuts
1 1/3 cups coconut

Cream butter and sugar in bowl until light and fluffy. Add eggs 1 at a time, mixing well after each addition. Add vanilla wafer crumbs alternately with milk, mixing well after each addition. Fold in walnuts and coconut. Batter may appear curdled. Pour into greased bundt pan. Bake at 350 degrees for 1 hour. Cool in pan for 15 minutes. Invert onto serving plate. Glaze cake or garnish with sprinkle of confectioners' sugar. Yield: 12 servings.

Approx Per Serving: *Cal 478; Prot 6.6 g; Carbo 51.9 g; T Fat 28.4 g; Chol 187.0 mg; Potas 162.0 mg; Sod 264.0 mg.*

Judy Fojtik
Ingleside, Illinois

5 eggs
2¹/₂ cups sugar
1 tablespoon butter
1¹/₄ cups milk, scalded
2¹/₂ cups sifted flour
¹/₈ teaspoon salt
2¹/₂ teaspoons baking
   powder
1 teaspoon vanilla extract
2 cups milk
¹/₂ cup sugar
¹/₂ cup flour
¹/₄ cup baking cocoa
¹/₃ cup milk
1 cup butter, softened
1 cup confectioners' sugar
2 teaspoons vanilla
   extract
1¹/₂ cups chopped pecans

Beat eggs in mixer bowl until light. Add 1 cup sugar gradually; mix well. Beat in 1¹/₂ cups sugar until light and fluffy. Combine 1 tablespoon butter and 1¹/₄ cups scalded milk. Stir until butter is melted. Cool to lukewarm. Add to egg mixture gradually; mix well. Sift in 2¹/₂ cups flour, salt and baking powder; mix well. Add 1 teaspoon vanilla; mix well. Pour into 2 waxed paper-lined 9x9-inch cake pans. Bake at 350 degrees for 25 to 30 minutes. Cool on wire racks. Split layers horizontally. Heat 2 cups milk in double boiler. Add mixture of ¹/₂ cup sugar, ¹/₂ cup flour, cocoa and ¹/₃ cup milk; mix well. Cook for 30 minutes or until thickened, stirring constantly. Remove from heat. Cool, covered, to room temperature. Cream 1 cup butter and confectioners' sugar in bowl until light and fluffy. Add to cooled mixture; mix well. Stir in 2 teaspoons vanilla. Spread between layers and over top and sides of cake. Sprinkle with pecans. Yield: 12 servings.

Approx Per Serving: *Cal 657; Prot 9.6 g; Carbo 87.6 g; T Fat 31.7 g; Chol 168.0 mg; Potas 240.0 mg; Sod 290.0 mg.*

Betty Zekan
Richfield, Ohio

OLDE VERMONTER BROWN SUGAR FUDGE

This is an ideal confection to give as a special holiday treat,
if the cook can keep from eating it all first.

3/4 cup butter
3 cups packed dark
  brown sugar
1 5-ounce can
  evaporated milk
1 teaspoon vanilla extract
1 16-ounce package
  confectioners' sugar
1/2 cup chopped walnuts

Combine butter, brown sugar and evaporated milk in saucepan. Bring to a boil. Cook over medium heat for 5 minutes, stirring frequently. Add vanilla, confectioners' sugar and walnuts; mix well. Pour into greased 9-inch square pan. Cool in refrigerator for 5 to 10 minutes. Cut into squares. Remove from pan. Yield: 36 squares.

Approx Per Square: *Cal 167; Prot 0.5 g; Carbo 30.8 g; T Fat 5.2 g; Chol 11.5 mg; Potas 85.1 mg; Sod 45.0 mg.*

Ginny Frye, Firewood Farm
Bristol, Vermont

PHIL WRIGLEY'S FUDGE

This was Philip K. Wrigley's way to relax. The fudge became so popular with
family and friends, it was known as "Phil's Phamous Phudge."

2 cups sugar
2 1-ounce squares
  unsweetened chocolate
1/2 cup milk
2 tablespoons butter
2 tablespoons corn syrup
1 teaspoon vanilla extract

"Bring all ingredients to a boil for approximately 6 minutes or until it forms a ball in a cup of cold water and starts to sugar around edge of pan. Let cool for a few minutes, then beat; when cooled further, add 1 teaspoon of vanilla. Tricky point is when to stop beating. If you stop too soon, it will be too soft; if too late, you cannot remove from pan. Recommend going by sound. As long as it goes clippity-clop, it is okay, but the minute it starts to sound like a cow pulling it's foot out of the mud, pour immediately into a buttered pan. Chill in the refrigerator. Let cool completely and remove from pan." Note: The amount of corn syrup used should vary according to weather. In hot, humid weather, use no syrup. In very dry weather, use 2 tablespoons syrup. Yield: 36 squares.

Approx Per Square: *Cal 62; Prot 0.2 g; Carbo 12.9 g; T Fat 1.3 g; Chol 2.2 mg; Potas 12.3 mg; Sod 8.0 mg.*

Misdee Wilson, Kaaba Arabian Enterprises
Scottsdale, Arizona

CARROT COOKIES

3/4 cup butter, softened
1 cup sugar
1 egg, beaten
1 cup mashed cooked
  carrots
2 cups flour
2 teaspoons baking powder
1/4 teaspoon salt
2 cups confectioners'
  sugar
1 tablespoon melted butter
1/2 teaspoon lemon juice
Grated rind of 1 orange
Juice from 1 orange

Cream 3/4 cup butter and sugar in bowl until light and fluffy. Add eggs; beat well. Add carrots alternately with mixture of flour, baking powder and salt; mix well. Drop by teaspoonfuls onto cookie sheet. Bake at 350 degrees for 10 to 12 minutes or until brown. Cool on wire rack. Combine confectioners' sugar, 1 tablespoon melted butter, lemon juice, orange rind and orange juice in bowl; mix until of spreading consistency. Spread on cookies. Yield: 36 cookies.

Approx Per Cookie: *Cal 116; Prot 1.0 g; Carbo 18.6 g; T Fat 4.4 g; Chol 18.8 mg; Potas 29.9 mg; Sod 73.1 mg.*

Jill S. Myles
Fort Collins, Colorado

CHOCOLATE DROP COOKIES

1 cup packed brown sugar
1/2 cup melted butter
2 tablespoons baking cocoa
1/2 cup milk
1 egg, beaten
1 teaspoon vanilla extract
1/2 teaspoon soda
1 1/2 cups flour
1/2 cup chopped raisins
1/2 cup chopped pecans

Combine brown sugar, butter and cocoa in mixer bowl; mix well. Add milk, egg and vanilla; mix well. Add mixture of soda and flour; beat well. Stir in raisins and pecans. Drop by teaspoonfuls onto greased cookie sheet. Bake at 375 degrees for 7 to 10 minutes or until brown. Cool on wire rack. Spread Chocolate Frosting on cookies. Yield: 18 cookies.

Approx Per Cookie: *Cal 233; Prot 2.4 g; Carbo 36.1 g; T Fat 9.6 g; Chol 33.8 mg; Potas 136.6 mg; Sod 91.3 mg.*
Nutritional information includes Chocolate Frosting.

Chocolate Frosting

1 cup sugar
2 tablespoons baking cocoa
2 tablespoons butter
1/4 cup milk
1/2 teaspoon cream of tartar
1/2 teaspoon vanilla extract

Combine sugar, cocoa, butter, milk, cream of tartar and vanilla in saucepan. Bring to a full boil. Remove from heat. Beat until of spreading consistency.

Syl Crooker
Mankato, Minnesota

CHRISTMAS COOKIES

1 cup sugar
1 cup packed brown
  sugar
1 cup butter, softened
2 eggs, beaten
2 tablespoons Amaretto
1 teaspoon baking
  powder
1 teaspoon soda
2 cups flour
1/2 teaspoon nutmeg
1/2 teaspoon cinnamon
3 cups oats
3 cups chopped pecans

Cream sugar, brown sugar and butter in mixer bowl until light and fluffy. Add eggs and Amaretto; mix well. Combine baking powder, soda, flour, nutmeg and cinnamon in bowl; mix well. Stir in oats and pecans. Add to sugar mixture; mix well. Roll into small balls; place on ungreased cookie sheet. Bake at 350 degrees for 12 to 15 minutes or until brown. Remove to wire rack to cool.
Yield: 60 cookies.

Approx Per Cookie: *Cal 129; Prot 1.8 g; Carbo 14.1 g; T Fat 7.6 g; Chol 17.4 mg; Potas 57.8 mg; Sod 49.3 mg.*

Helen McCoy, McCoy Arabians
Chino Hills, California

COUNTRY MORNING COOKIES

This recipe was originally on a box of cereal which is no longer available. I added extra raisins and dates.

1 1/2 cups packed brown
  sugar
1 1/2 cups margarine,
  softened
2 eggs, beaten
1 1/2 teaspoons vanilla
  extract
2 1/2 cups flour
3/4 teaspoon soda
1   16-ounce package oat
  cereal with raisins and
  dates
3/4 cup raisins
3/4 cup chopped dates

Beat brown sugar and margarine in mixer bowl until light and fluffy. Add eggs and vanilla; mix well. Add mixture of flour and soda; mix well. Stir in cereal, raisins and dates. Drop by level measuring tablespoonfuls onto cookie sheet. Bake at 350 degrees for 12 minutes or until brown. Cool slightly on cookie sheet. Remove to wire rack to cool completely.
Yield: 84 cookies.

Approx Per Cookie: *Cal 92; Prot 1.2 g; Carbo 12.6 g; T Fat 4.4 g; Chol 6.5 mg; Potas 68.2 mg; Sod 51.5 mg.*

Bliss Brown, Paramont Arabians
Abingdon, Virginia

DATE SQUARES

This is an old family recipe by my great grandma from Belgium.

1 8-ounce package
   dates, chopped
1 cup raisins
1½ cups water
½ cup sugar
1 cup packed brown
   sugar
1 cup shortening
1 egg, beaten
1 teaspoon vanilla extract
2½ cups 5-minute oats
2 cups flour
½ teaspoon salt
1 teaspoon soda
½ cup chopped walnuts

Combine dates, raisins, water and ½ cup sugar in saucepan. Simmer for 15 to 20 minutes or until mixture is of spreading consistency, stirring constantly. Remove from heat. Cool. Cream brown sugar and shortening in mixer bowl until light and fluffy. Add egg and vanilla; mix well. Combine oats, flour, salt and soda in bowl; mix well. Add to brown sugar mixture; mix well. Press half the brown sugar mixture into 9x13-inch baking dish. Spread with date filling. Crumble remaining brown sugar mixture over filling. Sprinkle with walnuts; press into crumbled dough. Bake at 350 degrees for 20 minutes or until brown. Cut into squares. Yield: 28 cookies.

Approx Per Cookie: *Cal 224; Prot 3.0 g; Carbo 33.8 g; T Fat 9.5 g; Chol 9.8 mg; Potas 171.0 mg; Sod 74.9 mg.*

Darlene M. Thomas, Rahza Thomas Arabians
Grand Rapids, Michigan

GRAHAM CRACKER PRALINES

Try to control yourself and don't eat them all at once.

24 graham crackers
1 cup packed brown
   sugar
1 cup unsalted butter
1 cup chopped pecans
1 teaspoon Amaretto

Line 10x15-inch cookie sheet with graham crackers. Combine brown sugar and butter in saucepan. Simmer for 3 minutes, stirring constantly. Stir in pecans and Amaretto. Spread over graham crackers. Bake at 350 degrees for 10 minutes. Cut into bars while warm. Cool on cookie sheet. Yield: 72 cookies.

Approx Per Cookie: *Cal 55; Prot 0.3 g; Carbo 5.1 g; T Fat 3.9 g; Chol 6.9 mg; Potas 23.8 mg; Sod 16.1 mg.*

Phil Witter, Live Oak Arabians
Baton Rouge, Louisiana

LEMON BARS

1 cup flour
1/2 cup margarine, softened
1/4 cup confectioners' sugar
2 eggs, beaten
1 cup sugar
3 tablespoons lemon juice
1/4 teaspoon salt
2 tablespoons flour
1 tablespoon confectioners' sugar

Combine 1 cup flour, margarine and 1/4 cup confectioners' sugar in bowl; mix well. Press into 8-inch square baking dish. Bake at 350 degrees for 15 to 20 minutes or until lightly browned. Combine eggs, sugar, lemon juice, salt and 2 tablespoons flour in bowl; mix well. Pour over baked crust. Bake at 350 degrees for 20 to 25 minutes or until set. Cool. Sprinkle with 1 tablespoon confectioners' sugar. Yield: 16 cookies.

Approx Per Cookie: *Cal 149; Prot 1.8 g; Carbo 21.4 g; T Fat 6.5 g; Chol 34.2 mg; Potas 22.9 mg; Sod 110.0 mg.*

Marilynn Hajek
Longmont, Colorado

MAPLE SYRUP COOKIES

1 egg, beaten
1/2 cup margarine, softened
1/2 teaspoon vanilla extract
1/2 cup maple syrup
2 cups flour
1/2 teaspoon soda
1/2 teaspoon salt
1/2 cup chopped pecans
1 cup confectioners' sugar
2 tablespoons butter, softened
1/4 cup maple syrup

Combine egg, 1/2 cup margarine, vanilla and 1/2 cup maple syrup in mixer bowl; beat well. Sift in flour, soda and salt; mix well. Stir in pecans. Drop by teaspoonfuls onto greased cookie sheet. Flatten with fork. Bake at 350 degrees for 10 minutes or until brown. Cool on wire rack. Combine confectioners' sugar, 2 tablespoons butter and enough remaining 1/4 cup maple syrup to make of spreading consistency. Spread over cookies. Yield: 36 cookies.

Approx Per Cookie: *Cal 94; Prot 1.1 g; Carbo 12.6 g; T Fat 4.5 g; Chol 9.3 mg; Potas 25.2 mg; Sod 79.3 mg.*

Theresa Ferland Blaisdell, Thistledown Farm
Lunenburg, Vermont

PEANUT BUTTER BARS

This easy, make-ahead recipe is sinfully delicious.

2 cups peanut butter
1/2 cup melted butter
1/2 cup packed brown
  sugar
1/2 teaspoon vanilla
  extract
2 1/2 cups confectioners'
  sugar
1 1/2 cups semisweet
  chocolate chips
2 tablespoons butter

Combine peanut butter, 1/2 cup melted butter, brown sugar, vanilla and confectioners' sugar in bowl; mix well. Press into 9x13-inch baking dish. Melt chocolate chips and 2 tablespoons butter in saucepan, stirring frequently. Spread over peanut butter layer. Chill in refrigerator until set. Cut into squares. Yield: 100 cookies.

Approx Per Cookie: *Cal 67; Prot 1.6 g; Carbo 5.8 g; T Fat 4.7 g; Chol 3.1 mg; Potas 48.5 mg; Sod 31.4 mg.*

Holly Andersen, Rorbeck Arabians
Willis, Texas

PEANUT BUTTER COOKIES

This recipe is good for people watching salt intake. The only salt is in the peanut butter. My grandsons love them.

1/2 cup unsalted butter,
  softened
1/2 cup peanut butter
1/2 cup sugar
1/2 cup packed brown
  sugar
1 egg, beaten
1/2 teaspoon vanilla
  extract
1/2 teaspoon soda
2 cups flour

Cream butter, peanut butter, sugar and brown sugar in mixer bowl until light and fluffy. Add egg, vanilla and mixture of soda and flour; mix well. Shape into walnut-sized balls. Place on cookie sheet; flatten with fork. May refrigerate before shaping into balls to stiffen dough. Bake at 350 degrees for 10 minutes or until firm. Cool on wire rack. Yield: 50 cookies.

Approx Per Cookie: *Cal 67; Prot 1.4 g; Carbo 8.3 g; T Fat 3.3 g; Chol 10.4 mg; Potas 32.0 mg; Sod 21.4 mg.*

Belle Walters
Acton, California

ROCK SPRINGS PEANUT BUTTER COOKIES

This easy recipe has served thousands at Kansas 4-H center at Rock Springs.

4 cups margarine,
  softened
4 cups sugar
2³/₄ cups packed brown
  sugar
8 eggs
4 cups peanut butter
11 cups flour
4 teaspoons soda
2 teaspoons salt

Cream margarine, sugar and brown sugar in large mixer bowl until light and fluffy. Add eggs; beat well. Blend in peanut butter. Sift in flour, soda and salt; mix well. Drop by teaspoonfuls onto greased cookie sheet. Flatten with fork. Bake at 300 degrees for 10 to 12 minutes or until golden brown. Cool on wire rack. Yield: 144 cookies.

Approx Per Cookie: *Cal 164; Prot 3.4 g; Carbo 18.1 g; T Fat 9.1 g; Chol 15.2 mg; Potas 79.1 mg; Sod 147.0 mg.*

Bill Riley
Manhattan, Kansas

PINEAPPLE COOKIES

¹/₄ cup butter, softened
¹/₂ cup sugar
¹/₂ cup packed brown
  sugar
1 egg, beaten
1 20-ounce can juice-
  pack crushed
  pineapple, drained
1¹/₄ cups flour
1¹/₂ cups oats
¹/₂ teaspoon soda
¹/₂ teaspoon salt
¹/₂ teaspoon cinnamon
¹/₂ teaspoon nutmeg

Cream butter, sugar and brown sugar in large mixer bowl until light and fluffy. Add egg and pineapple; mix well. Mix flour, oats, soda, salt, cinnamon and nutmeg in bowl. Add to butter mixture; mix well. Drop by teaspoonfuls onto cookie sheet. Bake at 375 degrees for 12 minutes or until brown. Cool on wire rack. Yield: 36 cookies.

Approx Per Cookie: *Cal 74; Prot 1.3 g; Carbo 13.8 g; T Fat 1.7 g; Chol 11.1 mg; Potas 48.3 mg; Sod 55.5 mg.*

Teresa H. Vinger
Reno, Nevada

AWARD-WINNING OATMEAL COOKIES

This recipe was entered as Ari's 4-H project for first-year members the summer of 1988. With the help of many practice sessions, Ari's efforts took a first-place ribbon in a class of 34. This is a must try recipe.

3 eggs
1 cup raisins
1 teaspoon vanilla extract
1 cup butter, softened
1 cup packed brown
  sugar
1 cup sugar
2½ cups flour
1 teaspoon salt
1 teaspoon cinnamon
2 teaspoons soda
2 cups oats

Combine eggs, raisins and vanilla in bowl. Let stand, covered, for 1 hour. Do not skip this step. Cream butter, brown sugar and sugar in mixer bowl until light and fluffy. Add flour, salt, cinnamon and soda; mix well. Stir in egg mixture and oats. Dough will be stiff. Drop by heaping teaspoonfuls onto greased cookie sheet. Bake at 350 degrees for 10 to 12 minutes or until brown. Cool on wire rack. Yield: 72 cookies.

Approx Per Cookie: *Cal 80; Prot 1.1 g; Carbo 12.4 g; T Fat 2.9 g; Chol 18.2 mg; Potas 42.7 mg; Sod 88.0 mg.*

Ari Anne Harvey
Lake Geneva, Wisconsin

OATMEAL-COCONUT COOKIES

This recipe came to me through the wife of a horse trainer working at an Arabian horse ranch in Lafayette, Louisiana, seven years ago.

1 cup packed brown
  sugar
1 cup sugar
1 cup butter
2 eggs
1 teaspoon vanilla extract
1 teaspoon soda
1 teaspoon salt
1 cup flour
1 cup coconut
3½ cups oats

Cream brown sugar, sugar and butter in mixer bowl until light and fluffy. Add eggs and vanilla; mix well. Add mixture of soda, salt and flour; beat well. Stir in coconut and oats. Drop by heaping teaspoonfuls onto cookie sheet. Bake at 350 degrees for 12 to 15 minutes or until brown. Cool on wire rack. Yield: 24 cookies.

Approx Per Cookie: *Cal 220; Prot 2.9 g; Carbo 30.6 g; T Fat 9.2 g; Chol 43.5 mg; Potas 54.4 mg; Sod 205.5 mg.*

Steve and Rebecca Galloway
Lexington, Kentucky

JOSIE'S RUSSIAN ROCKS

This was my great grandmother's recipe. It makes great gifts for friends at Christmas.

1 cup butter, softened
1½ cups sugar
3 eggs, beaten
2½ cups flour
1 teaspoon salt
1½ teaspoons cinnamon
1½ teaspoons allspice
1 teaspoon soda
1 tablespoon water
1 pound pecans, chopped
1   15-ounce package
    raisins

Cream butter and sugar in mixer bowl until light and fluffy. Add eggs; mix well. Add flour, salt, cinnamon and allspice; mix well. Dissolve soda in water; stir into batter. Stir in pecans and raisins. Drop by spoonfuls onto greased cookie sheet. Bake at 350 degrees for 15 minutes or until brown. Cool on wire rack.
Yield: 30 cookies.

Approx Per Cookie: *Cal 282; Prot 3.4 g; Carbo 32.1 g; T Fat 17.1 g; Chol 44.0 mg; Potas 186.0 mg; Sod 159.0 mg.*

Jane Ann McClain
Crockett, Texas

PENNSYLVANIA GERMAN SUGAR COOKIES

This is a traditional Pennsylvania German cookie, one of the most popular in our area.

6¾ cups packed light
   brown sugar
2 cups margarine
4 cups buttermilk
3 tablespoons soda
5 pounds flour

Cream brown sugar and margarine in large mixer bowl until light and fluffy. Add buttermilk and soda; mix well. Add flour; mix well. Chill, covered, overnight in refrigerator. Roll out dough to ¼-inch thickness on floured surface. Cut with 3½-inch round cookie cutter. Place on cookie sheet. Bake at 375 degrees for 15 minutes or until brown. Cool on wire rack.
Yield: 60 cookies.

Approx Per Cookie: *Cal 264; Prot 4.2 g; Carbo 48.6 g; T Fat 6.0 g; Chol 0.5 mg; Potas 135.5 mg; Sod 202.7 mg.*

Linda Manwiller, Tri-County Arabian Horse Club
Stouchsburg, Pennsylvania

OLD-FASHIONED SOFT SUGAR COOKIES

1/2 cup shortening
1 cup sugar
1 egg
1 teaspoon vanilla extract
1/2 cup sour cream
3 1/4 cups sifted flour
1 teaspoon soda
1/2 teaspoon salt
1 teaspoon nutmeg
3 tablespoons sugar

Cream shortening and 1 cup sugar in mixer bowl until light and fluffy. Add egg, vanilla and sour cream; mix well. Sift in flour, soda, salt and nutmeg; mix just until blended. Roll to 1/4-inch thickness on floured surface. Cut with cookie cutter; sprinkle with 3 tablespoons sugar. Place on cookie sheet. Bake at 425 degrees for 10 minutes or until brown. Cool on wire rack. Yield: 30 cookies.

Approx Per Cookie: *Cal 117; Prot 1.6 g; Carbo 17.6 g; T Fat 4.6 g; Chol 10.8 mg; Potas 20.0 mg; Sod 67.7 mg.*

Lisa Jo Marsh
Grand Blanc, Michigan

SOUR CREAM APPLE PIE

Although this pie contains no sour cream, it tastes as if it does.

3 tablespoons flour
3/4 cup sugar
1/8 teaspoon salt
1 cup whipping cream
1 egg, well beaten
1 teaspoon vanilla extract
1 teaspoon lemon juice
2 cups chopped peeled
   apples
1 unbaked 9-inch pie
   shell
1 cup flour
1/2 cup packed brown
   sugar
1/2 cup butter

Mix 3 tablespoons flour, sugar and salt in medium bowl. Combine whipping cream, egg, vanilla and lemon juice in mixer bowl; mix well. Add flour mixture gradually, stirring until smooth. Stir in apples. Spoon into pie shell. Mix 1 cup flour and brown sugar in small bowl. Cut in butter until crumbly. Sprinkle over pie. Bake at 425 degrees for 15 minutes. Reduce temperature to 350 degrees. Bake for 30 minutes longer. Cool. Yield: 6 servings.

Approx Per Serving: *Cal 712; Prot 6.5 g; Carbo 81.1 g; T Fat 41.3 g; Chol 141.0 mg; Potas 190.0 mg; Sod 395.0 mg.*

Shirley Lerum
Bieber, California

2 14-ounce cans
   sweetened condensed
   milk
8 egg yolks
1/2 cup whipping cream
7 ounces Key lime juice
1/3 cup shredded fresh
   coconut
1/2 teaspoon allspice
2 9-inch graham cracker
   pie shells

Combine condensed milk and egg yolks in mixer bowl; beat at low speed until well mixed. Whip cream in small bowl until soft peaks form. Blend into egg yolk mixture. Mix in lime juice gradually. Stir in coconut and allspice. Spoon mixture into pie shells. Chill in refrigerator overnight. Garnish with mixture of whipped cream and Amaretto. May top with meringue. Yield: 12 servings.

Approx Per Serving: *Cal 573; Prot 9.8 g; Carbo 71.8 g; T Fat 28.5 g; Chol 217.0 mg; Potas 368.0 mg; Sod 415.0 mg.*

Phil Witter, Live Oak Arabians
Baton Rouge, Louisiana

LEMON PIE

This easy recipe came from a girlfriend born and raised in the Giovanna Isles in Italy during World War II.

1 cup sugar
3 tablespoons cornstarch
1/4 cup butter, softened
1 tablespoon freshly
   grated lemon rind
1/4 cup fresh lemon juice
3 egg yolks
1 cup milk
1 cup sour cream
1 baked 9-inch pie shell

Mix sugar and cornstarch in saucepan. Add butter, lemon rind, lemon juice and egg yolks; mix well. Stir in milk. Cook over medium heat until thickened, stirring constantly. Cool. Fold in sour cream. Spoon into pie shell. Chill for 2 hours or longer. Garnish with whipped cream and nuts. Do not make substitutions for ingredients. Yield: 6 servings.

Approx Per Serving: *Cal 502; Prot 5.9 g; Carbo 54.4 g; T Fat 29.9 g; Chol 179.0 mg; Potas 150.0 mg; Sod 290.0 mg.*

Roberta Ashmore, Rubaiyat Arabians
Loomis, California

MINCEMEAT PIES

This traditional Pennsylvania German recipe has been in our family for at least 5 generations.

2 pounds pork
6 pounds beef
1 pound raisins
8 peeled apples
3/4 cup packed brown
   sugar
4 teaspoons cinnamon
2 3/4 teaspoons ground
   cloves
2 teaspoons allspice
3 1/2 teaspoons nutmeg
2 quarts dry Sherry
8 recipes 2-crust pie
   pastry

Cook pork and beef until tender. Trim fat. Cook raisins in water to cover for several minutes; drain, reserving liquid. Grind pork, beef and apples together. Mix in raisins and a small amount of reserved liquid. Stir in brown sugar, cinnamon, cloves, allspice, nutmeg, salt to taste and Sherry. Store in refrigerator for 4 days. Spoon into pastry-lined pie plates. Top with remaining pastry; seal edge and cut vents. Bake at 425 degrees for 10 minutes. Reduce temperature to 350 degrees. Bake for 50 minutes longer. Yield: 48 servings.

Approx Per Serving: *Cal 606; Prot 17.2 g; Carbo 38.4 g; T Fat 30.5 g; Chol 51.1 mg; Potas 343.0 mg; Sod 417.0 mg.*

Linda Manwiller, Tri-County Arabian Horse Club
Stouchsburg, Pennsylvania

KENTUCKY SINFUL PIE

This is my outrageously rich version of the famous Derby pie which used to be
served at the old Brown Hotel in Louisville. Although the Brown Hotel
is no longer there, her sinful desserts are immortal.

3 eggs, slightly beaten
1/2 cup packed dark
  brown sugar
1 cup light corn syrup
1 teaspoon vanilla extract
1 tablespoon Bourbon
1/4 teaspoon salt
11/2 cups pecan pieces
1/2 cup unsweetened
  shredded coconut
1 cup frozen semisweet
  chocolate chips
1 unbaked 9-inch pie shell
2 cups whipping cream,
  whipped
8 pecan halves

Combine eggs, brown sugar, corn syrup, vanilla, Bourbon, salt, pecan pieces, coconut and chocolate chips in bowl; mix well. Spoon into pie shell. Bake at 450 degrees for 10 minutes; reduce temperature to 350 degrees. Bake for 35 minutes longer. Cool. Top each serving with dollop of whipped cream and pecan half. Use Kentucky Bourbon. May omit Bourbon. I prefer frozen coconut because it is not so sweet. Yield: 8 servings.

Approx Per Serving: *Cal 835; Prot 8.2 g; Carbo 73.9 g; T Fat 60.5 g; Chol 184.0 mg; Potas 340.0 mg; Sod 282.0 mg.*

Linda White
Nicolasville, Kentucky

PECAN PIE

I have been making this very easy recipe for 25 years.
Everyone says it is the best they have ever eaten.

1 cup light corn syrup
1 cup packed dark brown
  sugar
1/3 teaspoon salt
1/3 cup melted butter
1 teaspoon vanilla extract
3 eggs, slightly beaten
1 cup pecans pieces
1 unbaked 9-inch pie
  shell

Combine corn syrup, brown sugar, salt, butter and vanilla in bowl; mix well. Mix in eggs. Stir in pecan pieces. Spoon into pie shell. Bake at 350 degrees for 40 to 45 minutes or until set. Yield: 6 servings.

Approx Per Serving: *Cal 700; Prot 6.5 g; Carbo 93.4 g; T Fat 36.3 g; Chol 164.0 mg; Potas 264.0 mg; Sod 461.0 mg.*

Judy Sirbasku
Waco, Texas

BACARDI PECAN PIE

This basic pie recipe is from "Fannie Farmer Baking Book" by Marion Cunningham. The Chantilly Cream recipe is from "Fast Fabulous Desserts" by Jack Lirio. I named this Bacardi Pecan Pie because this rum is by far the best!

3 eggs, well beaten
1 cup dark corn syrup
1/2 cup packed dark
  brown sugar
1/4 cup melted butter
1 tablespoon Premium
  Black Bacardi Superior
  rum
1 1/4 cups pecan halves
1 unbaked 9-inch pie
  shell
1 cup whipping cream
2 tablespoons
  confectioners' sugar
1 teaspoon vanilla extract

Combine eggs, corn syrup, brown sugar, butter and rum in medium bowl; beat until blended. Stir in pecan halves. Spoon into pie shell. Bake at 425 degrees for 15 minutes. Reduce temperature to 350 degrees. Bake for 15 to 20 minutes longer or just until set. Beat whipping cream and sugar in small mixer bowl until soft peaks form. Stir in vanilla. Serve pie warm with whipped cream on the side. May substitute additional rum for vanilla extract. Yield: 6 servings.

Approx Per Serving: *Cal 798; Prot 7.7 g; Carbo 79.8 g; T Fat 51.9 g; Chol 212.0 mg; Potas 242.0 mg; Sod 343.0 mg.*

Douglas B. Marshall, Gleannloch Farms
Barksdale, Texas

SOUR CREAM RAISIN PIE

The secret to the marvelous flavor and texture of my grandmother's raisin pie is the grinding of the raisins.

2 cups raisins, coarsely
  ground
1 cup sour cream
1/2 cup sugar
1/8 teaspoon salt
2 egg yolks
2 tablespoons flour
1 unbaked 9-inch pie
  shell
2 egg whites
1/2 cup sugar

Combine raisins and sour cream in top of double boiler. Cook over hot water for several minutes. Stir in 1/2 cup sugar and salt. Mix egg yolks, flour and enough water to make of pouring consistency in small bowl. Add to sour cream mixture; mix well. Cook until thickened, stirring constantly. Spoon into pie shell. Beat egg whites in small mixer bowl until stiff peaks form, adding remaining 1/2 cup sugar 1 teaspoon at a time. Spread meringue over top, swirling with back of spoon. Bake until lightly browned. Yield: 6 servings.

Approx Per Serving: *Cal 561; Prot 7.1 g; Carbo 93.8 g; T Fat 20.2 g; Chol 108.0 mg; Potas 508.0 mg; Sod 280.0 mg.*

Mary Anne Grimmell
Elk River, Minnesota

FROZEN RASPBERRY PIE

This very easy, make-ahead recipe is a family favorite.

1 10-ounce package
  frozen sweetened
  raspberries
1 cup sugar
2 egg whites
1 tablespoon lemon juice
1/8 teaspoon salt
1/2 cup whipping cream
1 teaspoon vanilla extract
1 baked 9-inch pie shell

Combine undrained raspberries, sugar, egg whites, lemon juice and salt in large mixer bowl; beat until stiff. Beat whipping cream and vanilla in medium bowl until stiff peaks form. Fold in raspberry mixture. Spoon into pie shell. Freeze for 3 hours to overnight. Garnish with whole raspberries or chocolate curls. May substitute other berries for raspberries. Yield: 6 servings.

Approx Per Serving: *Cal 401; Prot 3.7 g; Carbo 59.5 g; T Fat 17.4 g; Chol 27.2 mg; Potas 103.0 mg; Sod 256.0 mg.*

Janet Harlan
Arvada, Colorado

STRAWBERRY PIE

1 3-ounce package
  strawberry gelatin
1 cup boiling water
1 cup frozen strawberries
1/2 cup cold water
8 ounces whipped
  topping
1 8-inch graham cracker
  pie shell

Dissolve gelatin in boiling water in bowl. Add undrained strawberries and cold water. Chill until partially set. Beat for 1 minute or until frothy. Fold in whipped topping. Spoon into pie shell. Chill for several hours in refrigerator. Garnish with additional whipped topping and fresh strawberries. Yield: 6 servings.

Approx Per Serving: *Cal 405; Prot 5.2 g; Carbo 55.1 g; T Fat 19.2 g; Chol 3.8 mg; Potas 178.0 mg; Sod 389.0 mg.*

Clare Donoghue Beck
Goliad, Texas

After The Show

Quantity

HOT BROCCOLI AND CHEESE DIP

3 stalks celery, thinly
  sliced
1 medium onion,
  chopped
1 4-ounce can sliced
  mushrooms, drained
1/4 cup butter
3 tablespoons flour
1 5-ounce roll garlic
  cheese, sliced
1 10-ounce package
  frozen chopped
  broccoli, thawed
2 cans cream of celery
  soup

Sauté celery, onion and mushrooms in butter in skillet until tender. Add flour; mix well. Pour into lightly greased Crock•Pot. Add cheese, broccoli and soup; mix well. Cook on High until cheese melts, stirring occasionally. Cook on Low for 2 hours or until serving time. Serve hot from Crock•Pot or chafing dish with your favorite chips, crackers and assorted bite-sized fresh vegetables. Yield: 16 servings.

Approx Per Serving: *Cal 102; Prot 3.5 g; Carbo 6.3 g; T Fat 7.4 g; Chol 20.4 mg; Potas 132.0 mg; Sod 480.0 mg.*

Marge Spring
Tucson, Arizona

HAM AND SWISS APPETIZER SANDWICHES

1/2 cup butter
2 tablespoons instant
  onion flakes
1 1/2 teaspoons dry
  mustard
1 teaspoon
  Worcestershire sauce
1 1/2 teaspoons poppy
  seed
2 24-count packages
  dinner rolls
1 1/2 pounds thinly sliced
  deli ham
18 ounces Swiss cheese,
  sliced

Combine butter, onion flakes, dry mustard, Worcestershire sauce and poppy seed in small saucepan. Heat until butter melts, stirring frequently. Slice unseparated rolls into 2 layers. Layer bottom portions with ham and cheese slices; add tops of rolls to make 2 large sandwiches. Replace in foil roll pans. Drizzle butter mixture over tops. Bake at 350 degrees for 20 minutes. Cut rolls apart. Serve hot or at room temperature. Yield: 48 appetizers.

Approx Per Appetizer: *Cal 169; Prot 7.6 g; Carbo 15.0 g; T Fat 8.4 g; Chol 22.9 mg; Potas 99.1 mg; Sod 386.0 mg.*

Barbara Spring, Caravan Arabians
Santa Ynez, California

172

FRUITED CHICKEN AND RICE SALAD

1 cup slivered almonds
1 tablespoon butter
2 cups cooked long grain
  rice, chilled
2 cups finely chopped
  celery
1/4 cup finely chopped
  onion
2 cups green grape halves
2 8-ounce cans
  mandarin oranges,
  drained
10 cups chopped cooked
  chicken breasts
2 cups mayonnaise
1 to 2 cups ranch salad
  dressing

Sauté almonds in butter in skillet until golden; drain on paper towels. Combine rice, celery, onion, grapes, oranges and chicken in bowl; toss lightly to mix. Blend mayonnaise and desired amount of ranch dressing in bowl. Add to chicken mixture; mix lightly. Chill for 2 hours or until serving time. Spoon into large glass bowl lined with crisp lettuce leaves. Sprinkle almonds over top. Yield: 20 servings.

Approx Per Serving: *Cal 462; Prot 24.9 g; Carbo 15.2 g; T Fat 33.9 g; Chol 82.9 mg; Potas 347.0 mg; Sod 407.0 mg.*

Laurie Thomsen
San Luis Obispo, California

PENNSYLVANIA GERMAN POTATO SALAD

This is a traditional sweet and sour recipe that is a great family favorite.

3 pounds potatoes
6 to 8 slices bacon
2 eggs, beaten
1 cup sugar
1 cup water
1 cup cider vinegar
1 medium onion,
  chopped
1 cup chopped celery
3 or 4 hard-boiled eggs,
  chopped
2 carrots, grated

Cook unpeeled potatoes in water to cover in saucepan until tender; drain. Peel and coarsely chop potatoes. Fry bacon in large skillet until crisp; drain, reserving 1/4 cup bacon drippings. Beat eggs with sugar, water and vinegar in bowl. Add to hot reserved drippings in skillet. Cook until heated through, stirring constantly. Add potatoes, onion, celery, chopped eggs, carrots and crumbled bacon; mix well. Pour into large bowl. Chill overnight to allow flavors to season. Yield: 16 cups.

Approx Per Cup: *Cal 199; Prot 5.5 g; Carbo 37.0 g; T Fat 3.8 g; Chol 105.0 mg; Potas 476.0 mg; Sod 93.5 mg.*

Linda Manwiller, Tri-County Arabian Horse Club
Stouchsburg, Pennsylvania

WITCHES BREW

This recipe can be doubled and redoubled to serve many hungry people for trail rides or ski parties.

4 ounces bacon
1¹/₂ pounds ground beef
1 large onion, chopped
1 large green bell
  pepper, chopped
1 28-ounce can red
  kidney beans
1 28-ounce can tomatoes
1 4-ounce can button
  mushrooms
8 ounces noodles

Cook bacon in skillet until crisp; drain and crumble. Cook ground beef in skillet until brown and crumbly, stirring frequently; drain. Add bacon, onion, green pepper, beans, tomatoes and mushrooms; mix well. Bring to a simmer. Cook noodles in boiling water with 1 teaspoon salt in large saucepan for 15 minutes; drain. Add to ground beef mixture; mix well. Pour into casserole. Bake at 350 degrees for 30 minutes. Yield: 6 servings.

Approx Per Serving: *Cal 537; Prot 35.2 g; Carbo 37.9 g; T Fat 27.5 g; Chol 88.9 mg; Potas 1081.0 mg; Sod 1125.0 mg.*

Jo Ann Shea
St. Marys, Pennsylvania

GREAT BEANS

We love this recipe. We watch our fat intake and cholesterol count so we eat beans once a month. We eat beans for breakfast, too—a bean burrito with an egg on Sunday mornings is a treat!

1 pound dried beans
3 to 4 cups chicken stock
1 green bell pepper,
  chopped
1 onion, chopped
¹/₂ cup packed brown
  sugar
¹/₂ cup white cider
  vinegar
1 teaspoon crushed garlic
1 teaspoon sea salt
1 teaspoon dry mustard

Soak beans in water to cover in saucepan overnight. Place beans in Crock•Pot. Add stock, green pepper, onion, brown sugar, vinegar, garlic, salt and dry mustard; mix well. Cook on High for 6 hours. Reduce to Low if beans are tender or continue cooking on High. May add bacon or ham if desired. Add 1 cup salsa for a different flavor. I prefer Anasazi beans but any kind is good. Yield: 10 servings.

Approx Per Serving: *Cal 129; Prot 6.0 g; Carbo 25.2 g; T Fat 0.9 g; Chol 0.4 mg; Potas 394.0 mg; Sod 530.0 mg.*

Judith F. LaBounty
Glendora, California

BULGUR WHEAT BREAD

2 packages dry yeast
1/2 cup 115-degree water
1 cup dry bulgur wheat
3 cups boiling water
2 tablespoons corn oil
1 tablespoon salt
1/2 cup honey
6 to 7 cups unbleached
  flour
2 tablespoons butter

Dissolve yeast in warm water. Combine bulgur, boiling water, oil, salt and honey in large bowl; mix well. Let stand until cooled to lukewarm. Add yeast and enough flour to make medium dough; mix well. Knead on lightly floured surface until smooth and elastic. Place in greased bowl, turning to grease surface. Let rise, covered, until doubled in bulk. Shape into 3 loaves; place in greased loaf pans. Let rise until doubled in bulk. Bake at 350 degrees for 45 minutes or until loaves test done. Remove loaves to wire rack. Brush tops with butter. Yield: 36 slices.

Approx Per Slice: *Cal 133; Prot 3.2 g; Carbo 26.1 g; T Fat 1.7 g; Chol 1.7 mg; Potas 44.4 mg; Sod 184.0 mg.*

Linda Marshall
Boulder, Colorado

HUMMINGBIRD CAKE

3 cups flour
2 cups sugar
1 teaspoon salt
1 teaspoon soda
1 teaspoon cinnamon
3 eggs, beaten
1 1/2 cups oil
1 1/2 teaspoons vanilla
  extract
1   8-ounce can crushed
  pineapple
1 cup chopped pecans
2 cups chopped bananas
16 ounces cream cheese,
  softened
1 cup butter, softened
2 pounds confectioners'
  sugar
2 teaspoons vanilla
  extract
1 cup chopped pecans

Combine flour, sugar, salt, soda and cinnamon in large bowl. Add eggs and oil; mix just until ingredients are moistened. Add vanilla, undrained pineapple, 1 cup pecans and bananas; mix well. Spoon into 3 greased and floured 9-inch cake pans. Bake at 350 degrees for 25 to 30 minutes or until cake tests done. Cool in pans for 10 minutes; remove to wire rack to cool completely. Combine cream cheese and butter in mixer bowl; beat until creamy. Add confectioners' sugar; beat until light and fluffy. Add vanilla. Spread frosting between layers and over top and side of cake. Sprinkle 1 cup pecans over top. Yield: 12 servings.

Approx Per Serving: *Cal 1231; Prot 9.6 g; Carbo 146.0 g; T Fat 71.0 g; Chol 151.0 mg; Potas 297.0 mg; Sod 508.0 mg.*

Dawn Close
San Luis Obispo, California

WHITE FRUITCAKES

8 eggs, separated
2 cups butter, softened
2 cups sugar
1 2-ounce bottle of
   lemon extract
1/4 cup dark rum
3 1/4 cups flour
1 1/2 pounds candied
   cherries
8 ounces candied
   pineapple
1 pound pecans
1 pound white raisins
3/4 cup flour
1 cup orange juice
2 cups sugar
2 tablespoons grated
   orange rind
1/4 cup dark rum

Beat egg whites in mixer bowl until stiff peaks form; set aside. Cream butter and 2 cups sugar in mixer bowl until light and fluffy. Add egg yolks; beat well. Add lemon extract and rum; mix well. Add 3 1/4 cups flour; mix well. Combine candied cherries, pineapple, pecans and raisins in bowl. Add 3/4 cup flour; mix until fruit and pecans are coated. Add to batter; mix well. Spoon into 8 greased miniature loaf pans. Place pan of water in oven to keep cakes moist. Bake fruitcakes at 325 degrees for 1 hour or until toothpick inserted in center comes out clean. Combine orange juice, 2 cups sugar, orange rind and 1/4 cup rum in bowl; mix well. Prick tops of warm cakes with 2-pronged fork; drizzle orange juice mixture over cakes. Cool in pans. Yield: 8 fruitcakes.

Approx Per Fruitcake: *Cal 2056; Prot 20.4 g; Carbo 298.0 g; T Fat 91.3 g; Chol 398.0 mg; Potas 853.0 mg; Sod 467.0 mg.*

Marie Jo Anderson
Austin, Texas

MONSTER COOKIES

These cookies have gone to countless horse shows and trail rides over the years, sustaining numerous children (and adults!).

4 eggs
2 cups packed brown sugar
1 1/3 cups sugar
1 1/3 cups butter, softened
1 teaspoon corn syrup
1 teaspoon vanilla extract
1 tablespoon soda
1 teaspoon salt
16 ounces peanut butter
6 cups oats
6 ounces "M&M's"
   Chocolate Candies
8 ounces chocolate chips

Beat eggs in large bowl. Add sugars and butter; mix well. Add corn syrup, vanilla, soda and salt; mix well. Place in very large bowl or dishpan. Add peanut butter and oats; mix well with clean hands. Add candies and chocolate chips; mix well. Shape rounded teaspoonfuls into balls. Place 12 on each cookie sheet; flatten slightly with heel of hand. Bake at 350 degrees for 12 minutes. Cool on cookie sheet for 1 to 2 minutes. Remove to wire rack to cool completely. Yield: 144 cookies.

Approx Per Cookie: *Cal 81; Prot 1.8 g; Carbo 9.3 g; T Fat 4.5 g; Chol 12.2 mg; Potas 56.0 mg; Sod 63.6 mg.*

Marian Studer
Lexington, Kentucky

	Instead of:	Use:
Baking	1 teaspoon baking powder	1/4 teaspoon soda plus 1/2 teaspoon cream of tartar
	1 tablespoon cornstarch (for thickening)	2 tablespoons flour or 1 tablespoon tapioca
	1 cup sifted all-purpose flour	1 cup plus 2 tablespoons sifted cake flour
	1 cup sifted cake flour	1 cup minus 2 tablespoons sifted all-purpose flour
	1 cup fine dry bread crumbs	3/4 cup fine cracker crumbs
Dairy	1 cup buttermilk	1 cup sour milk or 1 cup yogurt
	1 cup heavy cream	3/4 cup skim milk plus 1/3 cup butter
	1 cup light cream	7/8 cup skim milk plus 3 tablespoons butter
	1 cup sour cream	7/8 cup sour milk plus 3 tablespoons butter
	1 cup sour milk	1 cup milk plus 1 tablespoon vinegar or lemon juice or 1 cup buttermilk
Seasoning	1 teaspoon allspice	1/2 teaspoon cinnamon plus 1/8 teaspoon cloves
	1 cup catsup	1 cup tomato sauce plus 1/2 cup sugar plus 2 tablespoons vinegar
	1 clove of garlic	1/8 teaspoon garlic powder or 1/8 teaspoon instant minced garlic or 3/4 teaspoon garlic salt
	1 teaspoon Italian spice	1/4 teaspoon each oregano, basil, thyme, rosemary plus dash of cayenne
	1 teaspoon lemon juice	1/2 teaspoon vinegar
	1 tablespoon mustard	1 teaspoon dry mustard
	1 medium onion	1 tablespoon dried minced onion or 1 teaspoon onion powder
Sweet	1 1-ounce square chocolate	1/4 cup cocoa plus 1 teaspoon shortening
	1 2/3 ounces semisweet chocolate	1 ounce unsweetened chocolate plus 4 teaspoons granulated sugar
	1 cup honey	1 to 1 1/4 cups sugar plus 1/4 cup liquid or 1 cup corn syrup or molasses
	1 cup granulated sugar	1 cup packed brown sugar or 1 cup corn syrup, molasses or honey minus 1/4 cup liquid

	When the recipe calls for:	Use:
Baking	½ cup butter	4 ounces
	2 cups butter	1 pound
	4 cups all-purpose flour	1 pound
	2½ to 5 cups sifted cake flour	1 pound
	1 square chocolate	1 ounce
	1 cup semisweet chocolate pieces	6 ounces
	4 cups marshmallows	1 pound
	2¼ cups packed brown sugar	1 pound
	4 cups confectioners' sugar	1 pound
	2 cups granulated sugar	1 pound
Cereal–Bread	1 cup fine dry bread crumbs	4 to 5 slices
	1 cup soft bread crumbs	2 slices
	1 cup small bread cubes	2 slices
	1 cup fine cracker crumbs	28 saltines
	1 cup fine graham cracker crumbs	15 crackers
	1 cup vanilla wafer crumbs	22 wafers
	1 cup crushed corn flakes	3 cups uncrushed
	4 cups cooked macaroni	8 ounces uncooked
	3½ cups cooked rice	1 cup uncooked
Dairy	1 cup shredded cheese	4 ounces
	1 cup cottage cheese	8 ounces
	1 cup sour cream	8 ounces
	1 cup whipped cream	½ cup heavy cream
	⅔ cup evaporated milk	1 small can
	1⅔ cups evaporated milk	1 13-ounce can
Fruit	4 cups sliced or chopped apples	4 medium
	1 cup mashed banana	3 medium
	2 cups pitted cherries	4 cups unpitted
	3 cups shredded coconut	½ pound
	4 cups cranberries	1 pound
	1 cup pitted dates	1 8-ounce package
	1 cup candied fruit	1 8-ounce package
	3 to 4 tablespoons lemon juice plus 1 tablespoon grated lemon rind	1 lemon
	⅓ cup orange juice plus 2 teaspoons grated orange rind	1 orange
	4 cups sliced peaches	8 medium
	2 cups pitted prunes	1 12-ounce package
	3 cups raisins	1 15-ounce package

	When the recipe calls for:	Use:
Meat	4 cups chopped cooked chicken 3 cups chopped cooked meat 2 cups cooked ground meat	1 5-pound chicken 1 pound, cooked 1 pound, cooked
Nuts	1 cup chopped nuts	4 ounces shelled 1 pound unshelled
Vegetables	2 cups cooked green beans 2½ cups lima beans or red beans 4 cups shredded cabbage 1 cup grated carrot 8 ounces fresh mushrooms 1 cup chopped onion 4 cups sliced or chopped potatoes 2 cups canned tomatoes	½ pound fresh or 1 16-ounce can 1 cup dried, cooked 1 pound 1 large 1 4-ounce can 1 large 4 medium 1 16-ounce can

Measurement Equivalents

1 tablespoon = 3 teaspoons 2 tablespoons = 1 ounce 4 tablespoons = ¼ cup 5⅓ teaspoons = ⅓ cup 8 tablespoons = ½ cup 12 tablespoons = ¾ cup 16 tablespoons = 1 cup 1 cup = 8 ounces or ½ pint 4 cups = 1 quart 4 quarts = 1 gallon	1 6½ to 8-ounce can = 1 cup 1 10½ to 12-ounce can = 1¼ cups 1 14 to 16-ounce can = 1¾ cups 1 16 to 17-ounce can = 2 cups 1 18 to 20-ounce can = 2½ cups 1 20-ounce can = 3½ cups 1 46 to 51-ounce can = 5¼ cups 1 6½ to 7½ -pound can or Number 10 = 12 or 13 cups

Metric Equivalents

The metric measures are approximate benchmarks for purposes of home food preparation.

Liquid	Dry
1 teaspoon = 5 milliliters 1 tablespoon = 15 milliliters 1 fluid ounce = 30 milliliters 1 cup = 250 milliliters 1 pint = 500 milliliters	1 quart = 1 liter 1 ounce = 30 grams 1 pound = 450 grams 2.2 pounds = 1 kilogram

GLOSSARY OF COOKING TECHNIQUES

Bake: To cook by dry heat in an oven or under hot coals.

Bard: To cover lean meats with bacon or pork fat before cooking to prevent dryness.

Baste: To moisten, especially meats, with melted butter, pan drippings, sauce, etc. during cooking time.

Beat: To mix ingredients by vigorous stirring or with electric mixer.

Blanch: To immerse, usually vegetables or fruit, briefly into boiling water to inactivate enzymes, loosen skin, or soak away excess salt.

Blend: To combine two or more ingredients, 1 of which is liquid or soft, to produce a mixture of uniform consistency quickly.

Boil: To heat liquid until bubbly; the boiling point for water is 212 degrees, depending on altitude and atmospheric pressure.

Braise: To cook, especially meats, covered, in a small amount of liquid.

Brew: To prepare a beverage by allowing boiling water to extract flavor and/or color from certain substances.

Broil: To cook by direct exposure to intense heat such as a flame or an electric heating unit.

Caramelize: To melt sugar in heavy pan over low heat until golden.

Chill: To cool in refrigerator or in cracked ice.

Clarify: To remove impurities from melted butter by allowing the sediment to settle, then pouring off the clear yellow liquid. Other fats may be clarified by straining.

Cream: To blend butter, margarine, shortening, usually softened with a granulated or crushed ingredient until the mixture is soft and creamy. It is usually described in the method as light and fluffy.

Curdle: To congeal milk with rennet or heat until solid lumps or curds are formed.

Cut in: To disperse solid shortening into dry ingredients with a knife or pastry blender. Texture of the mixture should resemble coarse cracker meal. Described in method as crumbly.

Decant: To pour a liquid such as wine or melted butter carefully from 1 container into another leaving the sediment in the original container.

Deep-fry: To cook in a deep pan or skillet containing hot cooking oil. Deep-fried foods are generally completely immersed in the hot oil.

Deglaze: To heat stock, wine or other liquid in the pan in which meat has been cooked, mixing liquid with pan juices, sediment and browned bits to form a gravy or sauce base.

Degorger: To remove strong flavors or impurities before cooking, i.e. soaking ham in cold water or sprinkling vegetables with salt, then letting stand for a period of time and pressing out excess fluid.

Degrease: To remove accumulated fat from surface of hot liquids.

Dice: To cut into small cubes about 1/4-inch in size. Do not use dice unless ingredient can truly be cut into cubes.

Dissolve: To create a solution by thoroughly mixing a solid or granular substance with a liquid until no sediment remains.

Dredge: To coat completely with flour, bread crumbs, etc.

Fillet: To remove bones from meat or fish. (Boneless piece of fish is called a fillet. Boneless meat or chicken piece is called a filet.)

Flambé: To pour warmed Brandy or other spirits over food in a pan, then ignite and continue cooking briefly.

Fold in: To blend a delicate frothy mixture into a heavier one so that none of the lightness or volume is lost. Using a rubber spatula, turn under and bring up and over, rotating bowl 1/4 turn after each folding motion.

Fry: To cook in a pan or skillet containing hot cooking oil. The oil should not totally cover the food.

Garnish: To decorate food before serving.

Glaze: To cover or coat with sauce, syrup, egg white, or a jellied substance. After applying, it becomes firm, adding color and flavor.

Grate: To rub food against a rough, perforated utensil to produce slivers, crumbs, curls, etc.

Gratiné: To top a sauced dish with crumbs, cheese or butter, then brown under a broiler.

Grill: To broil, usually over hot coals or charcoal.

Grind: To cut, crush, or force through a chopper to produce small bits.

Infuse: To steep herbs or other flavorings in a liquid until liquid absorbs flavor.

Julienne: To cut vegetables, fruit, etc. into long thin strips.

Knead: To press, fold, and stretch dough until smooth and elastic. Method usually notes time frame or result.

Lard: To insert strips of fat or bacon into lean meat to keep the meat moist and juicy during cooking. Larding is an internal basting technique.

Leaven: To cause batters and doughs to rise, usually by means of a chemical leavening agent. This process may occur before or during baking.

Marinate: To soak, usually in a highly seasoned oil-acid solution, to flavor and/or tenderize food.

Melt: To liquify solid foods by the action of heat.

Mince: To cut or chop into very small pieces.

Mix: To combine ingredients to distribute uniformly.

Mold: To shape into a particular form.

Panbroil: To cook in a skillet or pan using a very small amount of fat to prevent sticking.

Panfry: To cook in a skillet or pan containing only a small amount of fat.

Parboil: To partially cook in boiling water. Most parboiled foods require additional cooking with or without other ingredients.

Parch: To dry or roast slightly through exposure to intense heat.

Pit: To remove the hard inedible seed from peaches, plums, etc.

Plank: To broil and serve on a board or wooden platter.

Plump: To soak fruits, usually dried, in liquid until puffy and softened.

Poach: To cook in a small amount of gently simmering liquid.

Preserve: To prevent food spoilage by pickling, salting, dehydrating, smoking, boiling in syrup, etc. Preserved foods have excellent keeping qualities when properly prepared and then properly stored.

Purée: To reduce the pulp of cooked fruit and vegetables to a smooth and thick liquid by straining or blending.

Reduce: To boil stock, gravy or other liquid until volume is reduced, liquid is thickened and flavor is intensified.

Refresh: To place blanched drained vegetables or other food in cold water to halt cooking process.

Render: To cook meat or meat trimmings at low temperature until fat melts and can be drained and strained.

Roast: (1) To cook by dry heat either in an oven or over hot coals. (2) To dry or parch by intense heat.

Sauté: To cook in a skillet containing a small amount of hot cooking oil. Sautéed foods should never be immersed in the oil and should be stirred frequently.

Scald: (1) To heat a liquid almost to the boiling point. (2) To soak, usually vegetables or fruit, in boiling water until the skins are loosened; see blanch, which is our preferred term.

Scallop: To bake with a sauce in a casserole. The food may either be mixed or layered with the sauce.

Score: To make shallow cuts diagonally in parallel lines, especially meat.

Scramble: To cook and stir simultaneously, especially eggs.

Shirr: To crack eggs into individual buttered baking dishes, then bake or broil until whites are set. Chopped meats or vegetables, cheese, cream, or bread crumbs may also be added.

Shred: To cut or shave food into slivers.

Shuck: To remove the husk from corn or the shell from oysters, clams, etc.

Sieve: To press a mixture through a closely meshed metal utensil to make it homogeneous.

Sift: To pass, usually dry ingredients, through a fine wire mesh in order to produce a uniform consistency.

Simmer: To cook in or with a liquid at or just below the boiling point.

Skewer: (1) To thread, usually meat and vegetables, onto a sharpened rod (as in shish kabob). (2) To fasten the opening of stuffed fowl closed with small pins.

Skim: To ladle or spoon off excess fat or scum from the surface of a liquid.

Smoke: To preserve or cook through continuous exposure to wood smoke for a long time.

Steam: To cook with water vapor in a closed container, usually in a steamer or in a double boiler.

Sterilize: To cleanse and purify through exposure to intense heat.

Stew: To simmer, usually meats and vegetables, for a long period of time. Also used to tenderize meats.

Stir-fry: To cook small pieces of vegetables and/or meat in a small amount of oil in a wok or skillet over high heat, stirring constantly, until tender-crisp.

Strain: To pass through a strainer, sieve, or cheesecloth in order to break down or remove solids or impurities.

Stuff: To fill or pack cavities especially those of meats, vegetables and poultry.

Toast: To brown and crisp, usually by means of direct heat or to bake until brown.

Toss: To mix lightly with lifting motion using 2 forks or spoons.

Truss: To bind poultry legs and wings close to the body before cooking.

Whip: To beat a mixture until air has been thoroughly incorporated and the mixture is light and fluffy, volume is greatly increased, and mixture holds its shape.

Wilt: To apply heat causing dehydration, color change and a limp appearance.

COOKING MEAT AND POULTRY

ROASTING
- Use tender cuts of beef, veal, pork or lamb and young birds.
- Place meat fat side up, or poultry breast side up, on rack in foil-lined shallow roasting pan. Do not add water; do not cover.
- Insert meat thermometer in center of thickest part of meat, being careful that end does not touch bone, fat or gristle.
- Roast at 300 to 350 degrees to desired degree of doneness.

BROILING
- Use tender beef steaks, lamb chops, sliced ham, ground meats and poultry quarters or halves. Fresh pork should be broiled slowly to insure complete cooking in center. Steaks and chops should be at least 1/2 inch thick.
- Preheat oven to "broil". Place meat on rack in foil-lined broiler pan.
- Place meat on oven rack 2 to 5 inches from the heat source, with thicker meat placed the greater distance. Brush poultry with butter.
- Broil until top side is browned; season with salt and pepper.
- Turn; brown second side. Season and serve at once.

PANBROILING
- Use the same cuts suitable for broiling.
- Place skillet or griddle over medium-high heat. Preheat until a drop of water dances on the surface.
- Place meat in skillet; reduce heat to medium. Do not add water or cover. The cold meat will stick at first, but as it browns it will loosen. If juices start to cook out of the meat, increase heat slightly.
- When meat is brown on one side, turn and brown second side.

PANFRYING
- Use comparatively thin pieces of meat, meat that has been tenderized by pounding or scoring, meat that is breaded and chicken parts.
- Place skillet over medium high heat. Add a small amount of shortening— 2 tablespoons will usually be sufficient.
- When shortening is hot, add meat or poultry. Cook as in panbroiling.

BRAISING
- Use for less tender cuts of meat or older birds. You can also braise pork chops, steaks and cutlets; veal chops, steaks and cutlets; and chicken legs and thighs.
- Brown meat on all sides as in panfrying. Season with salt and pepper.
- Add a small amount of water—or none if sufficient juices have already cooked out of the meat. Cover tightly.
- Reduce heat to low. Cook until tender, turning occasionally. Meats will cook in their own juices.

COOKING IN LIQUID
- Use less tender cuts of meat and stewing chickens. Browning of large cuts or whole birds is optional, but it does develop flavor and improve the color.
- Brown meat on all sides in hot shortening in saucepan.
- Add water or stock to cover meat. Simmer, covered, until tender.
- Add vegetables to allow time to cook without becoming mushy.

NUTRITIONAL INFORMATION GUIDELINES

The editors have attempted to present these family recipes in a form that allows approximate nutritional values to be computed. Persons with dietary or health problems or whose diets require close monitoring should not rely solely on the nutritional information provided. They should consult their physicians or a registered dietitian for specific information.

Abbreviations for Nutritional Analysis

Cal — Calories	T Fat — Total Fat	Sod — Sodium
Prot — Protein	Chol — Cholesterol	g — gram
Carbo — Carbohydrates	Potas — Potassium	mg — milligram

Nutritional information for recipes is computed from information derived from many sources, including materials supplied by the United States Department of Agriculture, computer databanks and journals in which the information is assumed to be in the public domain. However, many specialty items, new products and processed foods may not be available from these sources or may vary from the average values used in these analyses. More information on new and/or specific products may be obtained by reading the nutrient labels.

Unless otherwise specified, the nutritional analysis of these recipes is based on the following guidelines.

- All measurements are level.
- Alternative ingredients are analyzed by the first named.
- Artificial sweeteners vary in use and strength so should be used "to taste," using the recipe ingredients as a guideline.
- Artificial sweeteners using aspertame (NutraSweet and Equal) should not be used in recipes involving prolonged heating which reduces the sweet taste. For details refer to package information.
- Alcoholic ingredients have been analyzed as used, although cooking causes the evaporation of alcohol thus decreasing caloric content.
- Buttermilk, sour cream, and yogurt are commercial-type.
- Chicken, cooked for boning and chopping, has been skinned and stewed; this method yields the lowest caloric values.
- Cottage cheese is cream-style with 4.2% creaming mixture. Dry-curd cottage cheese has no creaming mixture.
- Eggs are all large.
- Flour is unsifted all-purpose flour.
- Garnishes, serving suggestions and other optional additions and variations are not included in the analysis.
- Margarine and butter are regular, not whipped or presoftened.
- Milk is whole milk, 3.5% butterfat. Lowfat milk is 1% butterfat. Evaporated milk is produced by removing 60% of the water from milk.
- Oil is any cooking oil. Shortening is hydrogenated vegetable shortening. Fat for deep frying is not included in the nutritional analysis.
- Salt and other seasonings to taste as noted in the method have not been included in the nutritional analysis.

INDEX

BEYOND OATS...A HORSE LOVER'S COOKBOOK

All profits from **Beyond Oats...A Horse Lover's Cookbook** benefit the Arabian Horse Trust and Horse Clubs throughout the community.

Name_____

Address _____

City _____ State _____ Zip_____

Phone Number (____) _____

Item	Qty.	Unit Price	Total Price
Beyond Oats		$10.00 each	$
Beyond Oats Apron		$10.00 each	$
Beyond Oats Giftpack (includes cookbook and apron)		$18.00 each	$
Plus $1.00 postage and handling per item			$
Beyond Oats (case of 24) Apron FREE (mailed separately) Shipping FREE		$240.00 each	$
SUBTOTAL			$
Sales Tax (CO Residents Only) 3.7%			$
Additional tax deductible contribution			$
TOTAL AMOUNT			$

Enclosed is my check for $_____ (Payable to **Arabian Horse Trust**)

Charge to my   VISA____ MasterCard____

Account Number _____ Expiration _____

Signature _____

GIFT IDEA (Ship To) Please include personal message for each gift box.

Name_____

Address _____

City _____ State _____ Zip_____

Phone Number (____) _____

Items to ship _____

Name_____

Address _____

City _____ State _____ Zip_____

Phone Number (____) _____

Items to ship _____

ARABIAN HORSE TRUST   12000 Zuni Street   Westminster, CO 80234